GOLDEN
OF COLLEGE SPORTS
AGES

LONGHORN MADNESS

Great Eras in Texas Football

WILTON SHARPE

CUMBERLAND HOUSE
NASHVILLE, TENNESSEE

LONGHORN MADNESS
PUBLISHED BY CUMBERLAND HOUSE PUBLISHING, INC.
431 Harding Industrial Drive
Nashville, TN 37211-3160

Cover design: Gore Studio, Inc.
Text design: John Mitchell
Research assistance/data entry: Caroline Ross, Ariel Robinson

Content was compiled from a variety of sources and appears as originally presented; thus, some factual errors and differences in accounts may exist.

Library of Congress Cataloging-in-Publication Data

Sharpe, Wilton.
  Longhorn madness : great eras in Texas football / Wilton Sharpe.
    p. cm. — (Golden ages of college sports)
  Includes bibliographical references and index.
  ISBN-13: 978-1-58182-533-6 (pbk. : alk. paper)
  ISBN-10: 1-58182-533-1 (pbk. : alk. paper)
  1. Texas Longhorns (Football team)—History. 2. University of Texas at Austin—Football—History. I. Title. II. Series.
  GV958.T4S43 2006
  796.332'630976431—dc22

                                                          2006011903

Printed in the United States of America

1 2 3 4 5 6 7—12 11 10 09 08 07 06

For James "Jackrabbit" Saxton,
who ran like prairie wind

and

for Caroline,
loveUso

James "Jackrabbit" Saxton

CONTENTS

PREFACE

If you were to blow the dust off the 1962 yearbook of Cranwell School and happen upon the page of young Wilton Sharpe three-quarters through the broken-English brevity of yearbook thumbnails, you would light upon a descriptive line of unlimited promise:

"Alwoth, Tarkington, and Saxon all in one."

The fact that a fellow senior who was yearbook editor saw little need to proofread the final text enabled the above line to fly into posterity as is. Accurate translation: Alworth, Tarkenton, and Saxton all in one. That the claim was of high exaggeration was of small matter. When the editor had asked me, as the school's quarterback, to name my biggest football influences some months before publication, I didn't hesitate to toss out the names of three of my biggest heroes. Lance Alworth, a '61 senior at Arkansas, as everyone knows, turned out all right. Francis Tarkenton, then quarterbacking the Georgia Bulldogs...well, he had an okay career as a Hall of Fame quarterback in the far Norse woods. James Saxton, that consensus All-America senior halfback from the University of Texas who you never heard from again after his star-studded college days, was just about the finest broken-field runner you could ever hope to see, dazzling onlookers with his "jackrabbit" sojourns that mirrored the distinct look of a rabbit's trail and birthed a rightly earned nickname in the process (see more on page 113). If you were lucky, that meant watching Saxton in jaw-dropping awe crisscross back and forth across the grid prairie, sideline to sideline, a couple of times—darting, stopping, starting, dashing. Texas has had more productive and far more durable backs, but I doubt it ever had a more exciting one who consistently tore off the long landmark touchdown runs.

That was my introduction to Texas football. Since then, I've long since come to appreciate the tradition and winning tenure that engender the great football programs, and UT is certainly one of the true all-time kingpins. *Longhorn Madness* is the story of Texas football. It is a piece-by-piece rendering of the fabled UT football program, as told by the players, coaches, assistants, opponents, fans, and members of the media. It's Crain to Layne, Cotton to Campbell, Saxton to Appleton, Worster to Wuensch, Vince to Vasher, and all the exceptional Longhorns in between. It is humor and history, character and coaches, legendary feet and historical feats. If burnt orange courses through your veins, this book is for you.

It's all Longhorn.

— W. S.

LONGHORN TRADITION

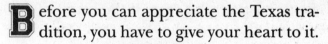

Before you can appreciate the Texas tradition, you have to give your heart to it.

Doug English
defensive tackle (1972–74)

To the surprise of the Texas contingent and more than 2,000 spectators, Texas defeated the highly rated Dallas Foot Ball Club by the score of 18–16 in the first-ever football game played in Texas.

Gene Schoor
author/sportswriter,
on the Thanksgiving Day game of 1893

—∼∼∼—

Jim Morrison, our tackle, had the honor of scoring the first touchdown in the history of Texas football. As we drove down-field, Ad Day, who carried the brunt of our attack, fumbled the ball, but Morrison caught it before it touched the ground and slashed through the Dallas players for the first touchdown in Texas football history.

Jesse Andrews
left guard, first University of Texas football
team, in 1893

HOOK 'EM HORNS

In 1955, Longhorn head yell leader Harley Clark Jr. was approached by a friend, Henry Pitts, who claims he invented the epic Hook 'Em Horns sign one night while making animal shadows on a dorm wall. Pitts asked Clark if he wanted to try out the new sign—an answer to Texas A&M's gig-'em, thumbs-up sign—at an upcoming Friday night pep rally, and Clark agreed to give it a shot.

The initial response was mild, with most students thinking the extended first-and-last-finger symbol corny. But the following day at Texas Memorial Stadium, in the Longhorns' game against Texas Christian, the entire stadium picked up on the novelty, flashing it continuously throughout the game. While the legendary sign took root that November 12 afternoon, it did little to stem Horned Frogs All-America halfback Jim Swink, who burned Texas for 235 rushing yards in a 47–20 TCU win.

Later, Clark would find out that the Hook 'Em sign carries different connotations. "If you flash it in Italy, it means your wife's sleeping around on you," noted Clark in Lou Maysel's *Here Come the Texas Longhorns*. "Somewhere else it means your mother's a dog."

Winning football games at Texas is a sacrament of such emotional intensity as to rival those of any other religion.

Gary Shaw
author/guard (mid-1960s)

———❦———

The history of Texas Longhorn football is like a great country and western music concert—there is a story behind every song.

Darrell Royal
head coach (1957–76)

———❦———

In 1903 a *Daily Texan* sports writer labeled the UT team "Longhorns." His name was D. A. Frank, a Texas student from 1903–05. Along about 1906 or 1907, the name became official.

Steve Richardson
author/writer

———❦———

hen you're born in Texas, you cut your teeth on football.

Bill "Rooster" Andrews
team manager/drop-kicker (1941–45)

Whatever the University of Texas football program is today is a direct result of Darrell Royal's insistence on doing things the right way.

Pat Culpepper
linebacker (1960–62)/
assistant coach (1963–64)

He *is* Longhorn football.

Douglas S. Looney
writer/author,
on Darrell Royal

I had a little diaper with a longhorn on it, and I've been wearing burnt orange and white ever since.

Jimmy Saxton
defensive back (1990–91),
son of 1961 consensus All-America halfback
James "Jackrabbit" Saxton

I'm proud of the fact that I'll always be a Longhorn. Once you're lucky enough to become part of the tradition here, you can't get it out of your system.

Jimmy Saxton

L ike "The Eyes of Texas," to experience the Texas Tower all dressed up in its best colors gives rise to goose bumps. Then there's Big Bertha, the world's biggest bass drum (eight feet in diameter), team mascot Bevo, a longhorn steer, and Smokey the Cannon.

Douglas S. Looney

—⟋⟋⟍—

P eople forget Bevo is a 2,000-pound animal. He's not tame. You just can't walk up to him and pet him whenever you want to. He might just give you a good pop with his horns. He lets you know who's in charge real quick.

Mike Kuhrt
former Silver Spurs
(honorary student organization) president,
on the UT mascot

I t seems he's as much a part of the game as the team.

Mike Kuhrt
on Bevo

—◦◦◦—

H e gets spooked by thunder and lightning and fireworks. People constantly get mad at us during the games because we won't let them near Bevo, but we're just being cautious. We've had so many near misses, but people still go after him like he's a stuffed animal.

Mike Kuhrt

Texas has tradition. That's whatever it is that makes you feel bigger than you are and faster than you are.

Fred Akers
assistant coach (1966–74)/
head coach (1977–86)

THE
BURNT ORANGE
& WHITE

*T*ime and memory tend to be selective when the short list of so-called "greats" is called. Too often, the unnoted player with the heart of a warrior goes unrecognized, lost in the shadow of a Vince Young, a Ricky Williams, an Earl Campbell, or a Tommy Nobis. Look beneath the hide of the Horns and you'll see the might that has earned Texas its preeminent niche in college football. Without them, the Burnt Orange & White could never have generated 27 SWC and Big 12 crowns, 45 bowl appearances, and three consensus national championships.

I n the fall of 1912, Clyde Littlefield entered the University of Texas and proceeded to carve out an athletic record in football, basketball, and track that has never been equaled at Texas.

Gene Schoor

FAST FACT: Littlefield, a halfback (1912–15), was called by esteemed sportswriter Grantland Rice "one of the greatest forward passing stars of the day."

—∿—

E rnie Koy was a 190-pound fullback who could run through a brick wall and was called upon whenever Texas needed that extra three or four yards for a first down; Koy was the man who delivered.

Gene Schoor

FAST FACT: Koy, the father of future UT stars Ernie Koy and Ted Koy in the 1960s, was a punishing back for the Longhorns from 1930 through 1932.

—∿—

B ohn Hilliard can do a lot of things that Red Grange couldn't do....I think before he is through here, he will go down as one of Texas's greatest backs.

Marty Karow
backfield coach (1927–35)

Mal Kutner, an end who became the first All-American from Texas, was recruited to play basketball.

John Maher
Kirk Bohls
authors

———— ᐧᐧᐧ ————

When Kutner came down here, he had so much athletic ability, he won a place in Mr. Bible's heart with his speed. [Assistant coach] Blair Cherry came up to Mr. Bible and said, "Let me have this guy. I could make a helluva end out of him."

Rooster Andrews
on the Longhorns' end from 1939 through '41

ROOSTER

Part mascot/part legend, Billy "Rooster" Andrews (1941–45) has become a treasured element of Longhorns lore.

A stocky but game figure of diminutive stature deemed too small to play football, Andrews became the first freshman student ever at Texas to make varsity football manager. He also was UT's best drop-kicker, a significant skill that found him converting occasional extra points for the Horns during his years at Texas. Adding to his unusual lore he once faked a drop-kick against TCU, throwing instead a pass to star quarterback Bobby Layne for the conversion. But it's the tale of the rooster that made Andrews a genuine UT folk hero.

One night during his freshman year, Andrews was rousted from his sleep by team pals intent on catching a rooster from a nearby university caretaker's tree that they might enter it in an early-morning illicit cockfight in nearby Elgin. It seems Andrews was volunteered to climb the tree and corral the rooster. The fowl turned foul, though, sending Andrews head over heels to the ground, bouncing off tree limbs along the way. The players got their cock and Andrews received a broken arm and colorful nickname for his troubles.

H e was very quiet and dedicated. He was a helluva punter, and he was always the mediator when we got into a fuss with someone. He'd always break it up. Maybe that was the coach coming out in him.

Hub Bechtol
*end (1944–46) and UT's first two-time
consensus All-American,
on Tom Landry (1947–48)*

T he best tobacco-chewing, snuff-dip-ping guard we ever had.

Bully Gilstrap
*end (1921–23)/assistant coach 1937–56),
on 1952 All-American Harley Sewell*

W alter Fondren was a neat guy. He was a good, steady quarterback. He kept everything in focus.

Ken Hall
*"The Sugar Land Express,"
legendary Texas schoolboy running back
(and briefly a Texas A&M halfback),
on the versatile UT
halfback/quarterback/receiver/kicker
of the mid-1950s*

I've never known a more intense person. He didn't laugh or smile two days before the game. I think he had a frown on his face from Wednesday on.

Knox Nunnally
end (1962–64),
on linebacker Johnny Treadwell

———

One of the most dynamic two-way players against OU, Johnny Treadwell tracked down running backs as a linebacker, blocked an extra point in UT's 9–6 win in 1962, and opened holes for his backs [as a guard].

Brian Davis
Chip Brown
Dallas Morning News

Treadwell and Pat Culpepper were two of the best linebackers I ever saw. Those two just loved goal-line defenses. They didn't care for this first-and-long stuff. They wanted you down there where you had to run right at them.

David McWilliams
defensive tackle (1961–63)/
assistant coach (1970–85)/
head coach (1987–1991)

—— ~~ ——

Culpepper was a pepperpot. Treadwell was just as intense, just quieter. He got so moody he wouldn't talk to people. But they would both step in there and meet a block.

Darrell Royal

David McWilliams was small for a defensive tackle, but he was as intense as he could be. He was lining up against people who weighed 235. He always managed to keep his body leverage and keep under 'em.

Darrell Royal
*on his over-achieving 188-pound co-captain
in 1963*

***

He's a rolling ball of butcher knives.

Pat Patterson
*assistant coach (1967–76),
on linebacker-guard Glen Halsell (1967–69)*

***

Jim Bertelsen, the physical sophomore halfback from Hudson, Wisconsin, had come to Texas because his aunt worked for a Grand Prairie dentist and Texas alumnus. Bertelsen combined 9.9 speed in the 100 with bone-pounding toughness. He tied the school record with four touchdowns against SMU [in 1969].

**John Maher
Kirk Bohls**

J im Bertelsen was as good an all-around player as we had. He could block, catch, get tough yardage, and be a break-away threat.

Donnie Wigginton
quarterback (1969–71)

> FAST FACT: *Bertelsen concluded his illustrious Longhorn career in 1971 with 2,510 rushing yards, then third-most in school history.*

R ick Ingraham was the toughest man I knew. He played his whole senior year on one leg. He needed a knee operation, but he'd hop around on one leg. I'd turn it up about six notches in a game. He'd turn his up about 44.

Earl Campbell
running back (1974–77),
on the Texas left guard from 1974
through '77

Marty was a little ol' cocky guy. Marty thought he was going to win every fight.

Spike Dykes
*assistant coach (1972–76),
on mid-'70s quarterback Marty Akins*

—〰—

I don't think Donnie Little got near the credit he deserved. You can't imagine some of the (hateful) calls and letters he got. But Donnie's a team person.

Fred Akers
*on the Texas quarterback
from 1978 through '81*

Bret Stafford was a good competitor. He could move around, and he was strong. If he had come along at a time when we had a good quarterback, he would have made a fine free safety. He was like Jerry Gray, but we couldn't afford to put him back there.

Fred Akers
*on the Texas quarterback who compiled 13
school passing records from 1984 through '87*

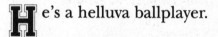

He's a helluva ballplayer.

Johnny Treadwell
*linebacker (1960–62),
on linebacker Winfred Tubbs (1989–90,
1992–93)*

He'd be a first-round pick if he were featured at some place like Miami.

Mel Kiper
*ESPN NFL draft expert,
on wide receiver Johnny Walker (1987–90)*

FAST FACT: Walker was drafted by the Green Bay Packers in the eighth round of the 1991 draft but failed to stick in the NFL.

THE APPLEWHITE-SIMMS
CONTROVERSY

The year following Texas quarterback Major Applewhite's selection as 1999 Big 12 Offensive Player of the Year as a sophomore, head coach Mack Brown and offensive coordinator Greg Davis, feeling the pressure of having signed Chris Simms, a major bluechip prep superstar with NFL pedigree credentials, generated a quarterback controversy in Austin that hadn't been seen since the late 1960s, when Super Bill Bradley was supplanted in the Wishbone by unheralded James Street.

After drawing the ire of critics for alternating Applewhite and Simms in 2000, Brown kicked it up a notch by announcing Simms as the starter for 2001 even before the season began. *The Sporting News* raised the bar further, hyping Simms as the next Heisman winner. Simms started 12 straight games that year, but in the 12th game—the 2001 Big 12 championship tilt against Colorado—Applewhite relieved an ineffective Simms and nearly pulled out a miraculous win in the narrow 39–37 loss to the Bisons.

Applewhite may have lost the war to Simms, but he won the last battle with an offensive MVP performance in the 47–43 Holiday Bowl victory over Washington concluding the 2001 season, passing for 473 yards and four touchdowns. With Simms a year behind Applewhite in eligibility, many Longhorn followers wonder why Brown and Davis made the decision they did.

Members of the Longhorn team had voted him Mr. GQ. His hair was blond and shined. His smile, perfect. His eyes, bright. He was a handsome young man whose face at once reflected the insouciant bearing of a stud athlete and the innocence of a back-country Opie.

W. K. Stratton
author/writer,
on quarterback Chris Simms (1999–2002)

—m—

He's a gifted athlete, and he just came out and played the game. Him coming in at running back shows what kind of talent he has.

Vince Young
quarterback (2003–05),
on wide receiver-turned-running back
Ramonce Taylor, who scored four touchdowns
and rushed for 102 yards in Texas's walloping
62–0 victory over Baylor in 2005

If the pocket is collapsing or a play is breaking down and Vince Young cannot save the day with his feet, the one guy he most wants to see is David Thomas. When the quarterback absolutely, positively needs someone to make the sure catch in the clutch, this is his guy.

Pat Forde
ESPN.com

—◊◊◊—

e gets me out of a lot of trouble.

Vince Young
*on All-Big 12 tight end David Thomas,
the Longhorns' leading receiver in 2005*

03

LONGHORN CHARACTER

The harder you work now, the easier the big games will be. You're going to love coming to the park on Saturday. Now get your tail moving.

Blair Cherry
*assistant coach (1937–46)/
head coach (1947–50)*

F ootball under Darrell Royal meant that you were taught to compete as hard as you could, to respect your opponents, to have loyalty to your teammates, and to play by the rules. You were always prepared, and whatever the outcome, you conducted yourself with class.

Jim Bob Moffett
tackle (1959–60)

—∽∾—

B efore Coach Mackovic came aboard, guys would pick up a chair and throw it at the wall, just go crazy. Now things are more business-like. If you need to rant and rave to get ready, something is wrong.

Van Malone
defensive back (1989–93)

—∽∾—

T exas football: It gave me a chance to make something of myself.

Earl Campbell

Freddie plays in a football game on Saturday, and on Monday he's taking X-rays. In less than week, he's lost his leg.

Darrell Royal
*on defensive back/punt returner Freddie
Steinmark, diagnosed with bone marrow
cancer in his leg after the 1969
Texas-Arkansas game*

—⁓—

Though the magnitude of the game is irrelevant, it bears repeating that six days after Freddie Joe Steinmark played in a football game, doctors told the world he had done it on a leg being eaten up by cancer. There never has been a more courageous effort on a football field. Ever.

Terry Frei
author/award-winning sportswriter

F reddie Steinmark is a great name to go down in the history of athletics at the University of Texas. I'm glad that scoreboard is there, named after him, and with a beautiful inscription.

Darrell Royal

FAST FACT: Steinmark, who lettered in 1968 and '69, died in 1971. The Royal-Memorial Stadium scoreboard is named in his honor.

Y ou just have to be realistic and take what comes along in life.

Freddie Steinmark

*safety (1968–69),
accepting the Philadelphia Sports Writers
Association's Most Courageous Athlete of the
Year award following his leg amputation
in December of 1969, one week after the
historic win over Arkansas in
The Big Shootout*

In the 1944 game against Arkansas, Bobby Layne had a temperature of 102. He had tonsillitis and was weak. So all he did was scramble for 44 yards and a TD. Then he tossed passes to Hub Bechtol and Leroy Anderson and kicked the conversion for all the points in a 19–0 win over the Razorbacks.

Rooster Andrews

If a dog is gonna bite you, he'll bite you as a puppy. If he's a striker and a fighter and a competitor, he was born that way. And a true winner has fought it all the way through, rising above his competitors. That's true in any field; if you're going to be successful, you've got to compete.

Darrell Royal

L ook around the room, and the one guy you spot getting all rowdy and loud, he's the one who will mess up by being overly aggressive.

Winfred Tubbs
linebacker (1989–90, 1992–93)

W e took great pride in our goal-line stands. As for the other team crossing our goal line, we just didn't want that to happen.

Johnny Treadwell
reflecting on what many have called the greatest goal-line stand in Longhorns history—against Arkansas in 1962 to preserve a 7-3 victory that led to Texas's first undefeated regular season since 1923

I won't accept what's good right now. I want us to achieve greatness.

Vince Young

Coach Royal taught me to learn the difference between injury and pain. If I was injured, I couldn't play. If I was in pain, I could go play.

Roosevelt Leaks
fullback (1972–74)

—∿∿—

If you stop to reflect on how cool this is, you'll lose and it won't be so cool anymore. So you better keep working and not look up.

Mack Brown
head coach (1998–),
to his 10–0 Longhorns in 2005, en route
to the school's third consensus national title,
but at the time Brown spoke, still with
three games to go

I was never nervous. That's not me. Nervousness, scariness, that's not even in our vocabulary.

Vince Young

after the undefeated No. 2-ranked Longhorns closed out the 2005 regular season with a challenging, come-from-behind 40–29 victory over Texas A&M

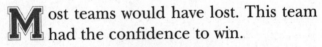

Most teams would have lost. This team had the confidence to win.

Mack Brown

following the 40–29 victory over Texas A&M in the 2005 regular-season finale

LONGHORN HUMOR

I was a split end in that great running/ non-passing offense. In most games, I was more likely to catch a cold than to catch a pass.

Cotton Speyrer
split end (1968–70),
on the Longhorns' use of the Wishbone
offense during Speyrer's days at Texas

Coach, if you ever turned on, would you do it with me? Would you promise me?

Willie Nelson
*to good friend Darrell Royal, an avowed
abstainer from marijuana*

——⁓——

In his brief acceptance speech, Earl Campbell said that when he was a small boy he would call on his mother when in trouble. Then turning to his mother, Earl said, "Well, Mom, I'm in trouble. Help me."

Gene Schoor
*on Campbell at the Heisman Trophy
ceremony at New York's Downtown
Athletic Club in November 1977*

——⁓——

Kids [today] have no idea who I am. They look at me like a goat looking at a new gate.

Darrell Royal

This is like parachuting into Russia.

Mike Campbell
assistant coach (1957–76),
enveloped in a sea of partisan, dressed-in-red
Razorback zealots prior to the 1965 game in
Fayetteville, Arkansas

—◊◊—

uper Bill was only Clark Kent.

Jones Ramsey
UT sports information director (1960–82),
on the impossible expectations placed upon
blue-chip super-soph quarterback Bill Bradley
in 1966

—◊◊—

If I could have just one strep throat to hand out, I'd give it to Jerry Levias.

Darrell Royal
his compliment to SMU's shifty receiving
threat prior to UT's 38–7 victory over the
Mustangs in 1968. Levias, the first African-
American football player to play in the
Southwest Conference, though double-
teamed by Texas, tallied six receptions for
124 yards

That was the wildest call since Billy Graham telephoned Zsa Zsa Gabor.

Cactus Pryor
co-host, The Darrell Royal Show,
on Royals's legendary fourth-and-3 call—
quarterback James Street's 44-yard pass to
Randy Peschel—that put Texas in position to
win The Big Shootout over Arkansas in 1969

D. X. Bible had such presence. He always made inspiring pregame speeches. I remember before the SMU game in '45, he made his usual inspirational talk. Jimmie Plyler, our captain, said, "Let's go, men." We were on slick concrete. Jimmie took off, and his feet slid out from under him. We couldn't get out of the room fast enough. That was slapstick comedy if you ever saw it.

Peppy Blount
end (1945, 1947–48)

Bobby Layne would bet on anything. He'd bet on a raindrop or on two ants crossing a windshield. He and I had a bet that each of us could wear the same underwear longer. It came out in a dead heat. We both went about 20 straight days. Anywhere we went, we had plenty of room.

Peppy Blount

—◦◦◦—

I don't know. We've never thrown him out of a second-story window.

Mike Campbell

in response to a Dallas Cowboys
questionnaire in the early 1960s that asked
Campbell if he threw halfback James Saxton
out a second-floor window, would the running
back land on his feet like a cat

No Favorites

Following Texas's huge win over Arkansas in the classic 1969 Big Shootout in Fayetteville, game hero and tight end Randy Peschel attempted to return to normal student life back on the Austin campus. His big-play 44-yard pass reception from quarterback James Street on fourth down-and 3 late in the fourth quarter had set up the Longhorns' winning touchdown and kept alive UT's drive for a national title.

Arriving for his statistics class the following Monday, Peschel took his seat as the instructor spoke briefly to the class about the accomplishments of teamwork, how individuals are subordinate to team play in the kind of game Texas had won the previous Saturday. All student eyes bored in on Peschel. The professor then quietly took off his sports coat and turned to face the blackboard for the first teaching task of the day. Emblazoned on his back was a homemade number 40—Peschel's jersey number. The antic brought the house down. "The class just went bonkers," said Peschel.

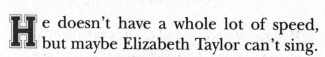

He doesn't have a whole lot of speed, but maybe Elizabeth Taylor can't sing.

Darrell Royal

on Harold "Lassie" Philipp (1962–64),
Ernie Koy's replacement at fullback in 1963,
after the Longhorn star suffered a shoulder
injury punting against Oklahoma State

The Texas Longhorns ran like there was an outhouse in each end zone.

Blackie Sherrod

longtime dean of Dallas sportswriters,
after Texas ran through Baylor for 555 total
yards in its 1969 defeat of the Bears, 56–14

---

e're going to the Toilet Bowl.

Kenneth Sims

defensive tackle (1978–81)/
two-time consensus All-American,
on the disappointment of the 1980
Texas team's 7–5 record and UT's subsequent
invitation to the Bluebonnet Bowl

Might as well reserve Bevo's guest spot with Jay Leno now and prepare Rodeo Drive for another invasion of cowboy boots.

Pat Forde

detecting the smell of roses following No. 2 Texas's 52–17 rout of No. 10-ranked Texas Tech to go 7–0 during the 2005 national championship season

I know 12 people who won't have any trouble sleeping tonight—Earl and the 11 guys who were trying to tackle him.

Darrell Royal

following Texas's 35–21 victory over Houston in 1977, in which Campbell ground out 173 rushing yards and three touchdowns despite suffering from a virus

He looks like he needs worming.

Darrell Royal

on slightly built split end Cotton Speyrer

LONGHORN LEGENDS

L ike a retired undefeated heavyweight champion, James Street's legend grew. There is no equal to Street's brinkmanship in the annals of Texas football. He was the fourth-down phantom, a gutsy gambler with all the confidence of a champion. He never lost a game. Starting at quarterback in 19 games through the 1968 and '69 seasons, Street brought Texas a second national championship.

Gene Schoor

A Texan darts through. Your breath stops. "Lordie, if that is Crain again, he may be off." It was Crain. He was gone a second time. The Texans in the stands were on their feet on a hysterics jag.

Bus Ham
Oklahoma City Oklahoman,
on Jack Crain's one-man show in Texas's
24–12 loss to Oklahoma in 1939. Crain scored
on 69- and 72-yard runs, the latter a record
from scrimmage in the series until 1947

—m—

D arrell Royal told me once I hit him harder than anyone. He said that more than once.

Hub Bechtol
who faced the future Texas head coaching
legend in the 1946 OU game

The only way to evaluate Bobby Layne is to say he was electric.

D. X. Bible

—◊—

If Bob Fenimore is All-America, Bobby Layne is All-Universe.

Fort Worth Star-Telegram,
1946

FAST FACT: Fenimore was a 1945 consensus All-America half-back from Oklahoma A&M.

—◊—

Bobby Layne was a great passer the first two years. Then, he decided he was going to toss the ball real fast. He had to bullet it and got in that habit. But he had great touch.

Hub Bechtol

—◊—

Bobby Layne is right up there at the top. If I had to choose a quarterback, Bobby would be it. He's just the greatest competitor who ever came down the pike.

Peppy Blount

Bobby had to fight for everything he got from the time he was eight years old. He got that attitude that you've got to fight like hell, and he never lost it. That's what made Bobby go—his competitive spirit. It didn't matter if he was playing washers, horseshoes, tiddly winks, or shuffleboard, he wanted to whip your ass.

Rooster Andrews

—◊◊◊—

He had confidence. He was not fast, but people had a hard time catching up with him. I just think he had natural ability. I really think Bobby Layne was probably the greatest athlete at the University of Texas.

Rooster Andrews

Bobby Layne

I do not believe that our Lone Star State has ever produced a better athlete than Bobby Layne. He was as fine a competitor as I've ever seen or ever hope to see.

Dana X. Bible
head coach (1937–46)

———〰———

Bobby Layne could do more things when he got half-popped. Did he drink before games? I'd be fibbin' if I told you different.

Rooster Andrews

———〰———

The big surprise [of 1947] was the play of halfback Tom Landry after Coach Cherry moved him into the fullback post. Landry gained 91 yards on 12 carries to spark a 34–0 rout of the North Carolina Tar Heels.

Gene Schoor

FAST FACT: *Landry went on to a fine six-year career as a punter/defensive back with the New York Giants and later gained Hall of Fame status as the 29-year head coach of the Dallas Cowboys.*

The 250-pound McFadin, who played both offense and defense in his final game, finished his career at Texas with a tremendous number of honors. He was picked on 15 All-America teams and was named winner of the Knute Rockne Memorial Trophy.

Lou Maysel
author/longtime Austin American-Statesman
sports editor, columnist,
on the Texas guard from 1948 through '50.
The Rockne award was given annually to the
top college lineman in the country

—m—

He was the toughest man who ever played for the Longhorns

Frank Medina
longtime UT trainer,
on All-America middle guard Harley Sewell,
who played from 1950 through '52

Harley Sewell was the most consistent lineman I've ever seen.

J. T. King
UT assistant coach (1950–52, 1954–56)/
Texas Tech head coach (1961–69),
on Texas's 6–1, 220-pound guard from St. Jo

—◊◊◊—

Sewell had the highest pain threshold and lowest percentage of mental errors of nearly any lineman who has played at Texas, trainer Frank Medina once said.

John Maher
Kirk Bohls

—◊◊◊—

People talk about Bud McFadin, Scott Appleton, and Tommy Nobis, but Harley Sewell was the toughest boy since I have been here. He was the most indestructible player as well as the most consistent. There were never any hot or cold days for Harley. He established a norm and kept it.

Frank Medina

Scott Appleton is the best defensive lineman I've had since I've been coaching
football. He makes tackles from sideline to
sideline; he's like blocking a wall on one
play and smoke the rest.

Darrell Royal

—⚭—

Scott Appleton was more of a finesse
guy—not that he wouldn't put a hit on
you. But he would slip blocks, jump this
way and jump back in and completely get
free and make a tackle. Nobis would just
knock the blocker down.

David McWilliams

He played every inch to his capabilities. An athlete cannot help it if he isn't 6'4" and weighs 250 pounds or can run under 10 seconds. The only things of which he has 100 percent control are aggressiveness, desire, and effort. Pat Culpepper mastered these things. And that's the most complimentary thing you can say about a boy.

Darrell Royal

John Treadwell could hit you with a forearm. But Nobis just had the instinct for finding the ball.

David McWilliams

Tommy Nobis is a one-man wrecking crew.

Darrell Royal

He was the most unselfish team player I've ever had the pleasure of working with at Texas, and he loved to hit.

Mike Campbell
on Tommy Nobis

I followed Texas football as a kid and had dreams of someday making the team, of being an All-American and playing with a Texas team that won the championship. I keep pinching myself about all the great things that have happened to me under Coach Royal and his staff. I can't quite believe it all. And now this year, 1965, I'm captain of a team that won the national championship. It's a far cry for a kid from Jefferson City who weighed 140 pounds and worried about making the high school team.

Tommy Nobis
linebacker (1963–65)

Tommy Nobis

If we were going to have a winning team, we were going to spend most of our time on offense. If Nobis played just defense, he's going to be out there just half the time. You gotta be crazy having Nobis play less than half the game.

Darrell Royal

—〰—

He was the most accurate tackler I'd ever seen. I don't know how he put himself in such good position. Very few ball-carriers went forward after he got them. He made more solid tackles than anybody I'd ever seen.

Darrell Royal
on Tommy Nobis

E rnie [M.] Koy is the greatest punter in the nation, college or pro. He averages 48 yards per kick and hangs the ball in the air for five seconds every time he boots one. Texas does not attempt to punt out of bounds. The Longhorns want the defense to handle the ball, figuring sooner or later some unfortunate safety man will fumble in the middle of a knot of Texas tacklers.

Red Blaik
legendary Army head coach,
on the Horns' star wingback/fullback/
tailback/punter of the early-to-mid 1960s,
son of UT's famous three-time All-SWC back
of the same name in the early 1930s

—∿—

I wanted to run the football like (fellow Palestinian) James Saxton. Nobody could jitterbug like him.

Bill Bradley
quarterback/defensive back (1966–68)

B ill Bradley was one of the best athletes I've ever seen. If he'd played his whole career at defensive back, he probably would have held the school record for interceptions. He could play quarterback, wide receiver, defensive back, and punter. He could throw the ball with either hand. He probably could have played basketball at Texas.

Jim Helms
running back (1964–66)

I f you tear Bradley's jersey off, you'll find a big red S on his t-shirt.

Doak Walker
immortal 1940s SMU halfback,
1948 Heisman Trophy winner, and
Pro Football Hall of Famer,
who tagged sensational Texas schoolboy
prospect Bill Bradley with the nickname
"Super Bill," during practice for the Big 33
Texas high school all-star game against
Pennsylvania in the summer of 1965

Bill Bradley would have been more successful if he had been in the right spot quicker. He was absolutely tremendous. He had tremendous jumping ability. If we'd had him on defense, he would have been everybody's All-American.

Darrell Royal

—◇◇◇—

The best athlete was Bill Bradley. Bill could do more things better than anyone I ever saw. Bradley was recruited by every school in the Southwest Conference for football, basketball, baseball, and track. He was also a great punter.

Fred Akers

—◇◇◇—

Street's biggest quality was his leadership. He had the ability to motivate. James never looked back. It was like a boulder rolling down a mountain.

Chris Gilbert
tailback (1966–68)

James Street wasn't Joe Montana, but he was a darn good athlete and made good decisions on the field.

Chris Gilbert

―~―

He'd get so excited, tears would be coming down his face. One time we were in the huddle and he said, "OK, on two. Break!" Well, he was so pumped up, he had forgotten to call a play. He had to call a timeout.

Chris Gilbert

on quarterback James Street

―~―

Steve Worster was excellent at finding daylight. He had good vision of where the soft spots were and great leg drive to drive through arm tackles.

Darrell Royal

You'd have to be a blind man not to be impressed by him.

Bo Hagan

*former Rice coach,
on fullback Steve Worster, after UT's 45–21
victory over Rice in 1970, in which Worster
ground out 170 yards, as Texas rushed an
all-time Longhorn high of 85 times. Later in
the season, against Arkansas, they upped the
mark to 90 rushes, an SWC record*

***

He's kinda like that 400-pound gorilla: He'll play wherever he wants to.

Darrell Royal

*asked where he planned to use much-
fanfared fullback recruit Steve Worster in
1968. The Horns already boasted a backfield
of halfbacks Chris Gilbert and Ted Koy,
indicating that Worster, a high school
tailback, would likely be used at fullback*

Before he had finished at Texas, Steve Worster rushed for 2,353 yards and won All-America honors. Then in 1971, Rosey Leaks took over at fullback in the Texas Wishbone offense and raised the power level a full notch. Leaks rushed for 2,514 yards, including a Southwest Conference record 1,415 yards in 1973 when he made the All-America team.

Gene Schoor

—∿—

Charles "Cotton" Speyrer, a 168-pound wisp from Port Arthur, blossomed forth in the fall of 1968. A blue-chip schoolboy halfback, his speed and quickness, so reminiscent of that of James Saxton, marked him as perhaps a super talent.

Lou Maysel

Jerry Sisemore was just fantastic. In the offseason, if you wanted to play pickup basketball, you'd pick Sisemore. He was so quick and good. He was just an athlete.

Donnie Wigginton

on the Longhorns' all-time offensive tackle from 1970 through 1972, at the time only the second two-time consensus All-American in Texas history

—◆—

If Jerry Sisemore's mother had been more thoughtful and just had triplets.

Darrell Royal

—◆—

Brad Shearer didn't win that trophy (Outland, 1977) by accident. Brad was an outstanding defensive tackle. He enjoyed everything. He had a good sense of humor. He didn't take himself too seriously. He would compete, especially against the run. He was awfully tough on those offensive linemen.

Fred Akers

Steve McMichael never thought any-body could beat him at anything. He was a handful....He was a warrior, a battler, like Brad Shearer.

Fred Akers

—〰—

I thought Steve McMichael was one of the outstanding competitors in college football. I don't think I've ever seen a guy whom football meant more to than Steve. He'd find a way to get mad during a game.

Fred Akers

on Texas's first two-time consensus
All-America defensive tackle (1976–79)

—〰—

Russell Erxleben set school records with four field goals against TCU and broke Bill Bradley's career punting average with a 44.2-yard mark.

John Maher
Kirk Bohls

the Longhorns' all-time punter/placekicker
(1975–78) also hit an NCAA-record 67-yard
field goal against Rice in 1977, later tied by
Arkansas' Steve Little

By 1979, his senior season, Johnny "Lam" Jones already held six Texas receiving and touchdown records, including most TD passes in a career (12), longest touchdown kickoff return (100 yards), and best average yardage per catch (25 yards).

Gene Schoor

—✺—

Lam may be the fastest football player in the world.

Darrell Royal

—✺—

Johnny is the fastest player I've ever seen or coached. We know he's fast, we've never even bothered to time him.

Fred Akers

on Johnny "Lam" Jones, a 1976 Olympic
4x100 relay gold medalist and Longhorns
wide receiver from 1976–79

He's offset a little bit to the left. Eleven yards from tying the record . . . Williams breaks the hole. Williams—hello record book—Ricky Williams runs to the Hall of Fame! Cut back. Ricky Williams . . . touchdown! . . . Sixty yards and the record is his. He did it in dramatic fashion. And a standing ovation for the king of the rushers.

Brent Musburger

ABC play-by-play broadcaster, his call on Williams's record-breaking run against Texas A&M in 1998, establishing the all-time NCAA career mark for most yards rushing, breaking Tony Dorsett's 23-year-old record. On the day against the Aggies, Williams lugged the ball a career-high 44 times for 259 yards

Roy Williams's athletic ability has no equal in college football. I try to get him the ball in good spots so he can make plays. Roy can go one on one with anybody. I can throw it up, and at 6'5" with long arms, he can jump out of the stadium.

Chris Simms

quarterback (1999–2002),
on the Horns' talented wide receiver from
2000 through 2003

—〰—

For the Orangebloods, Cedric Benson's first snap from scrimmage had been awaited with only slightly less anticipation than the second coming of Earl Campbell. Or Jesus. Take your pick.

W. K. Stratton

on the super bluechip Texas recruit who went
on to become the Longhorns' second-leading
rusher of all time and the No. 1 draft pick
of the Chicago Bears in 2005

LEGENDARY COACHES

The numbers still generate gasps. Rolled into one brilliant package, Darrell Royal was Picasso and Mozart and Einstein and Rockne and Patton and Churchill and John Wayne and Thomas Jefferson; he was also Willie Nelson and a 35-foot sidehill putt for a birdie and a sunset over Maui.

Douglas S. Looney

His practices were so rough that one of his players called him "The Prussian Field Marshall." Many nights, after a grueling practice session, Chevigny and his coaches, dead tired after hours on the field, would simply collapse and fall asleep in the coach's office, too tired to go home.

Gene Schoor
on head coach Jack Chevigny (1934–36)

—◊◊◊—

Jack Chevigny initiated several notable improvements in the overall football program. He began to film all games and had a small studio set aside so his coaches could study film. He also made arrangements to house the football squad in a dormitory. He believed that it would make for a more unified group and help develop a new spirit of togetherness.

Gene Schoor

I n 1937, Dana X. Bible accepted a ten-year contract [as Texas head coach], worth anywhere from $15,000 to $20,000 per year. That was more than twice what the school president made.

Gene Schoor

—⁓—

D . X. Bible has a firm hold on Texas hearts. He coached from 1937 to '46 and was so respected that, to this day, everyone—and that definitely includes one Darrell Royal—refers to him as Mr. Bible. Every time.

Douglas S. Looney

—⁓—

H e's as confident as a banker and as astute as a schoolmaster.

Joel Hunt
Texas A&M halfback (1927),
on then-Aggie head coach Dana X. Bible

Bible was one of the greatest psychologists I've ever known. You could be down and beat, but he could get you to forget that game and get you ready for the next one. He was always using different quotations and examples. Bible knew how to get an athlete's mind into thinking positive.

Jack Crain
halfback (1939–41)

Anybody can swim downstream. You've got to swim against the current if you're going to be a champion.

Dana X. Bible

A thoroughbred doesn't have to have a dry track.

Dana X. Bible

Coach Bible established the program without any question. He brought it back from oblivion. It wouldn't be near what it is without him.

Hub Bechtol

D. X. Bible was a coach everybody could respect. You could look up to him kind of like you did your preacher.

Mal Kutner
end (1939–41),
UT's first-ever All-American

—◊◊◊—

Coach Cherry was the most underrated and one of the greatest coaches the University of Texas will ever have. He wore his feelings on his cuff and let fans get on him. He should have been more mentally tough.

Peppy Blount

—◊◊◊—

Football was good to me. I don't know of another profession in which I—starting out as a penniless lad compelled to make his own way—might have risen to the top of his field and had as much fun doing it.

Blair Cherry

There never was a Texan as beloved as Oklahoma's Darrell Royal.

Cactus Pryor

———〰———

There's nothing natural about football. Watch people Christmas shopping. They'll have an occasional bump but they very carefully try to avoid each other. That's the natural thing to do....So how unnatural is it for guys in football to back off and run into each other at high speeds? There's nothing natural about that. And there wasn't anything natural about those Japs flying down those smokestacks, either. That's all mental. You've got to have people psyched up to do that.

Darrell Royal

O ne of the first and most important fac-
tors in a successful business is a good
public relations man. First and foremost,
that is Coach Royal. This public relations
ability requires characteristics that we usually think of as belonging to an adroit
politician.

Gary Shaw

I would hate to have him for an opponent in a political race because he
attends to every little detail, he doesn't
make mistakes, and he wins nearly every
time he comes to bat.

John Connally
former Texas governor,
on Darrell Royal

N ot mean, fair.

James Street
quarterback (1968–69),
on Coach Royal

Those of us who have spent considerable time around Darrell Royal know that there is no more frustrating undertaking than trying to get Darrell to say something he has no intention of saying. The harder you press and the more contentious you become, the cooler, the calmer, the more imperturbable Royal becomes.

Roy Edwards
former sportswriter, Dallas Morning News

—— ᨑ ——

I found out real early in coaching that I needed the press. I didn't need to fight the press. The press had a job to do, and I had a story to tell, so we needed to work together.

Darrell Royal

—— ᨑ ——

I 'd steal a hot stove for him.

Dwight Jefferson
defensive end (1976–78)/district court judge in Harris County, Texas

I think above all what probably separates Darrell Royal from less successful coaches is his superior ability to play on the fears of boys in their late adolescence.

Gary Shaw

———

His inability to speak before large groups held him back as an assistant coach, so he memorized poems and turned his natural gift for observing human nature into a knack for saying the right thing at the right time, usually in a short and witty sentence.

Pat Culpepper
on Darrell Royal

———

He had the right chin.

Cactus Pryor
on Royal

ROYALISMS

I'm on the right side of dirt.

—⟋⟍—

If worms had pistols, birds wouldn't eat 'em.

—⟋⟍—

That putt there is as close as one is to two.

—⟋⟍—

You can't win a peeing contest with a skunk.

—⟋⟍—

There ain't a hoss that can't be rode and there ain't a man that can't be throwed.

—⟋⟍—

We're gonna dance with who brung us.

Olde Saying
popularized by Royal, on sticking with what works well for you

A great runner—a Chris Gilbert or a James Saxton or Earl Campbell—would turn three-yard runs into forty, sixty yards. As the other team wears down, if you are superior, what starts out in the first quarter as two-, three-, five-yard gains becomes six, seven, ten, fifteen yards. I mean, those runs get bigger as it goes into the fourth quarter, when you start to dominate, if you're better.

Darrell Royal

A lot of our big ball games were won throwing, but the Wishbone was a good offense. I don't know whether it'd go in today's market or not. I don't care.

Darrell Royal

They talk about the Wishbone, they say that you can't come from behind; that it's not any good when you're behind with two minutes to go. My rebuttal to that is you're supposed to be doing something the first 58 minutes. The object of your game is not to be behind with two minutes to go.

Darrell Royal

—〰—

Emory Bellard came up with the idea [of the Wishbone]. He was the backfield coach here then, and he came up with the alignment and the way we'd run it. It was his idea. But Mickey Herskowitz named it.

Darrell Royal

The University of Texas

Darrell Royal

You don't run into people unless you're geared up. You have to get psyched up to run into people and knock folks around enough to come out on the long end of the score. That's the reason you can't scrimmage every day. If people really enjoyed doing this, you'd go out and scrimmage every day. But they really don't enjoy it. So why do they do it? For recognition. That's the only reason a guy plays football.

Darrell Royal

—∿∿—

I say football doesn't build character. Football is a process that eliminates the weak of character while making those with real character even stronger.

Darrell Royal

If you use the team approach too much, a player can use that as a dodge. He can say the team wasn't ready. But you can't dodge behind that any more than if you're successful you can walk in there and claim, "I did it alone."

Darrell Royal

If guys didn't play for recognition, you could give 'em nice sports coats at the end of the season instead of letter jackets. They wouldn't stand still for that for five minutes, because that letter jacket is a badge of honor. They're proud of it, and they ought to be. Our players just love to show off those national championship rings—and who can blame them?

Darrell Royal

I 'm not really a football fan. But I am a fan of people, and I am a Darrell Royal fan because he is the rarest of human beings.

Lyndon B. Johnson
36th president of the United States

H e knew what buttons to push.

Gary Shaw
on Darrell Royal

I think if he would leave, it would be like taking Bevo from the Longhorns.

Anonymous fan
on rumor of Darrell Royal's retirement during the 1976 season finale against Arkansas

I can't say which straw made the camel go down on his knees....I've used up a lot of ammunition. I always felt I wanted to quit before I was totally spent, while there was still a little ham on the bone.

Darrell Royal
*on retiring as head coach following the 1976
season at age 52, after 20 years at Texas*

—◊◊◊—

It has been so long ago that it seems like maybe I didn't do what I did. I do know it was a dream I didn't dream. I'm in the debt of Texas. I'll never get it repaid. I walked through a rainstorm my whole career, but somehow I never got wet.

Darrell Royal

ABC-TV network conducted a poll of the nation's sportswriters to select the leading college football coach of the 1960s. Darrell Royal was voted Coach of the Decade.

Gene Schoor

———〰———

Greatest coach of the last 50 years— Darrell Royal.

Frank Broyles

longtime Arkansas head coach, whose years in Fayetteville coincided with Royal's in Austin

———〰———

I always appreciated Darrell Royal for giving me the chance to get into college football. I learned a lot from Darrell. You learn things by copying them, and you learn things you don't want. I studied him and learned from him.

Fred Akers

I detected one thing about him. He didn't mess around. It's strictly business with him.

Earl Campbell
on Fred Akers

———❦———

F red Akers had a dominant personality. He used to say, "It's okay to think you're better than the rest because you are. You're going to play well because you're a Texas Longhorn." For some reason, that's interpreted as being pompous. But success breeds success. I always thought that was a great quality in him.

Jeff Ward
placekicker (1983–86)

———❦———

T here was no doubt in his mind. He brought such confidence to the team. We were not going to lose. Whenever he stepped on the field, he never felt we were going to lose.

Brad Shearer
defensive tackle (1974–77),
on Fred Akers

He was an eternal optimist. That was the best thing about Fred Akers.

Jeff Ward

—⁓—

We couldn't have hired Knute Rockne and got people more excited.

"Mack" Rankin, Jr.
*UT alumnus,
on the hiring of David McWilliams as Texas
head coach in 1987*

—⁓—

Mike Campbell could get a yellow pad, watch every film of an opponent, and not a word would be spoken. Then, when it was over, he'd say, "OK, here's what we're going to do." It was always so simple.

David McWilliams
*on 20-year Longhorn assistant coach
Campbell, whom many felt should have been
the rightful successor to Darrell Royal*

I don't care how witty or how dramatic you are as a speaker, the pregame talk is useless if you haven't done a good job preparing the team in practice.

John Mackovic

I'm always amazed at how calm Coach Mackovic is whenever he talks to the team. He can motivate you without yelling. If he raises his voice even a little, you really know he means business.

Joey Ellis
cornerback (1991–94)

Football is not dancing.

John Mackovic

That's the next Darrell Royal right there.

Earl Campbell
on Mack Brown

———♒———

I doubt that our current football coach, Mack Brown, would have come to Texas had he not had the blessing of DKR.

Cactus Pryor

———♒———

We said, "How lucky are we? We've got a good team and a chance to do something we haven't done." That's exciting. You have to embrace that here. Enjoy the moment. Enjoy being Texas football players.

Mack Brown
on his 2005 Longhorns

———♒———

When you come to a place like Texas, I don't think you know truly what you're into. I think I've grown into the job.

Mack Brown

No question Mack's done a great job at Texas of unifying their people and maximizing what they've done over there. He's brought Coach Royal back into the program, embraced the former players at Texas, and done a great job of selling their tradition.

R. C. Slocum
former Texas A&M head coach,
on Mack Brown

—))(—

When somebody talks about your coaches and players, it's like someone talking about your mother.

Vince Young

—))(—

Upon taking the Texas job in late 1997, Mack Brown was called by Ohio State coach John Cooper "the Number 1 program-builder in college football."

Tim Layden
writer, Sports Illustrated

He's relaxed, not uptight. He'll get on you if you drop a ball or make a mistake, but he jokes around, asks about your family or your girlfriend.

Vince Young
on Mack Brown

———

He tells you, "Life is bigger than football." Then he says, "Just go out and play and don't worry about things." Guys want to play for a coach like that.

Derrick Johnson
linebacker (2001–04),
on Mack Brown

———

Very few coaches get to decide where they want to finish. And that's a real pressure point for a coach in his 50s and 60s, when he doesn't have a place to stop. You don't know where you're gonna be buried.

Mack Brown

That took a big monkey off his back. I think this is an opportunity to quiet all of the people who have criticized him in the past. Winning a conference championship was a goal we set a long time ago.

David Thomas
tight end (2002–05),
on Mack Brown, following the 2005 Big 12
title game rout of Colorado, Brown's first-ever
conference championship

—◊—

Coach Royal told me a story that really scared me my second year at Texas: There is not a team that your fan base doesn't think you should beat. And if you're not careful, he said, you get so you're relieved after a win and devastated after a loss. And you don't have any joy.

Mack Brown

I t finally allowed him to shed the label of being college football's version of soap opera diva Susan Lucci.

Tim Griffin
*San Antonio Express-News/ESPN.com,
on Mack Brown,
after the Texas coach won his first-ever
conference championship in the 70–3
obliteration of Colorado in the 2005 Big 12
championship game*

—∿—

L ast year, when Texas athletic director DeLoss Dodds gave Mack Brown a 10-year contract extension, Brown didn't make the speech Sally Field made when she won her second Best Actress Oscar—"You like me! You really like me!"—but the extension had the same effect.

Ivan Maisel
ESPN.com

IN-VINCE-IBLE

His teammates catalog favorite VY moments. . . . They're just waiting for the day their kids and grandkids ask them what it was like to play with the immortal Vince Young.

Eric Neel
ESPN the Magazine

Obviously he's a great runner. Tonight he showed us he's a great passer.

A. J. Hawk

*Ohio State All-America linebacker,
on quarterback Vince Young, following UT's
25–22 come-from-behind win over the
Buckeyes in September 2005. Young passed
for 270 yards and two touchdowns and
rushed for 76 yards in the game*

Vince's performance was the best today that I've ever seen.

Mack Brown

*after Young's 2005 performance against
Colorado, in which the Longhorns' QB
finished with 394 total yards and a career-
high 336 passing yards, including 16-of-18
for 258 yards in the first half. His 86.2
completion percentage rate—25-of-29—set a
Texas record*

He just takes off and adds another dimension, and it kills us.

Jordan Dizon
Colorado linebacker

—⧟—

His passing is night and day from last year. It was pretty embarrassing. They really put it to us.

Nick Reid
Kansas linebacker,
on Vince Young, following the Jayhawks'
humiliating 66–14 loss to Texas in 2005.
During that contest, Young became UT's
career total offense leader with 8,269 yards,
breaking the school record of 8,059 set by
Major Applewhite (1998–2001)

—⧟—

I'm the guy, and I'm going to be the leader. That's my role.

Vince Young
2005 Maxwell Award winner and the only
player in NCAA history to rush for 1,000
yards (1,150) and pass for 3,000 yards (3,038)
in a single season

I was telling him sometimes what 50 Cent be saying; it's similar to some of our guys' lives.

Vince Young

as part of a group of Texas players who went to coach Mack Brown and urged him to listen to some hip-hop music that the players like. Brown says he downloaded the music himself into his iPod digital music player

—⟋∭⟍—

There's been a couple of times we got caught standing around and he's still back there running. It gives us a lot of confidence to know there's a playmaker back there. When the chips are down, he can pull something from nowhere.

Justin Blalock

tackle (2003–06), on Vince Young

Vince Young

The University of Texas

THE CONVERSION
OF BILL SIMMONS

During the dramatic 2005 national championship game victory over Southern Cal, ESPN.com Page Two writer Bill Simmons jotted down his thoughts as Texas came from behind in a shocker to win the 2006 Rose Bowl, headed by Vince Young's metaphorical athleticism. Early in the game, Simmons, fully expecting to see mighty USC take its third straight national crown, began his dagger-throwing at Texas's No. 10.

"Let's be honest—there's no way Vince can succeed in the NFL with that throwing motion. It's impossible, I'm telling you. There has never been a successful NFL quarterback who threw like that. And by "that," I mean, throws like someone who just realized they have dog poop on their hand and is trying to fling it off."

Later in the first half, Simmons fired another poison-tipped barb at Young's throwing style:

"Hey, after the game, do you think Vince Young will give Johnny Damon his throwing arm back?"

Midway through the third quarter Young scampered 14 yards for a touchdown that put UT up 23–17.

"Screw it, why couldn't some NFL team just run the option with Vince? Wouldn't you rather have him running your team than Charlie Frye or J. P. Losman?"

Late in the third quarter, Young scrambled 45 yards to the USC 20, giving him 150 yards on the night (and counting).

"Wow. This guy could throw like Costner's Dad in 'Field of Dreams' and still thrive in the NFL. Unbelievable. He's killing USC. Now I would put him above Frye, Losman, Gus Frerotte, Brooks Bollinger, Kyle Orton, Mike McMahon, David Carr, Josh McCown, Joey Harrington, Patrick Ramsey, Kyle Boller, and all the Detmers. And we're not even in the fourth quarter yet."

With USC holding on at 38–33, the game came down to Texas's final play: fourth-and-5 from the Southern Cal 8-yard line.

"Young lines up behind center as Keith Jackson chuckles, 'I'm too old for this.' The snap, some pressure, Young has to scramble . . . touchdown, Texas! Wait, can I swear on ESPN.com? Because that was [bleeping] unbelievable! Vince Young, everybody! He's just joined the 200–200 club. 'You're not gonna beat him!' Dan Fouts screams. 'Invincible!'"

With Texas ahead by one point, 39–38, Simmons awaited the Longhorns' two-point conversion attempt with just over 20 seconds remaining in the game, his conversion to full-fledged UT admirer complete.

"Young runs for the 2-point conversion. I now have him ranked above every NFL QB except for Tom Brady, Peyton Manning, and Carson Palmer."

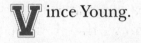

Vince Young.

Cedric Benson
tailback (2001–04),
when asked the secret behind the Longhorns'
good karma during UT's 2004 season

—⧟—

The guy's a character. He's so confident and he just knows he's going to make something happen. It's just a matter of time.

Neale Tweedie
tight end (2003–06),
on Young

—⧟—

He makes it look so easy, like everything is in slow motion. It just seemed like another workmanlike day for him.

Mack Brown
on Vince Young, after Texas's 62–0
annihilation of Baylor, November 5, 2005,
in which Young completed 16-of–27 passes for
298 yards and a pair of touchdowns and
rushed for an additional 53 yards on just
eight carries

Everything Vince does is great for our team. Vince does things that I think not too many people can do.

Michael Griffin
safety (2003–06)

That's an extraordinary football player. He was obviously the difference in the game. He's really off the charts.

Pete Carroll
*USC head coach,
on Young's Rose Bowl MVP performance
that knocked off Southern Cal in the 2005
national championship game, in which the
gifted Texas QB produced a "200–200"
game—running for 200 yards and passing
for another 267 yards to set a Rose Bowl
record for total offense (467 yards)—in UT's
41–38 victory*

He just breaks teams' backs.

Mack Brown
on Young

I'm loose. I get that drive, that beat, and I'm dancing before it's even game time.

Vince Young
*who led the nation in passing efficiency
(168.6) in 2005*

—⟋⟍—

He's the best quarterback in the country. The bigger the scene, the better he likes it.

Mack Brown
on Young

—⟋⟍—

Vince Young's legs set him apart from the exceptional pocket passers at USC and ND. His leadership has been immeasurable to the Longhorns, and he's the clearest team MVP in the nation. It's hard to envision Texas being much better than 8–3 without him.

Pat Forde

—⟋⟍—

He's embraced here like no one I've ever seen.

Mack Brown
on Young

The guy is magnetic. You're just drawn to him. I've seen him morph into the best player in the country.

David Thomas
on Young

———〰———

He just takes over a game. Just like he did in the 2005 Rose Bowl. Seeing him take over a game like he did against Michigan, you saw the coming of a great player. He hasn't slowed down since then.

Gary Barnett
former Colorado head coach,
on Vince Young

———〰———

Vince has worked hard at being a complete quarterback. The game has slowed down for him now. He's beyond the thought process. He's running through progressions, making decisions without dwelling on the steps.

Greg Davis
offensive coordinator/quarterbacks coach
(1998–)

Vince is what the NFL demands now, with the sophisticated defenses we see. You need the ability to run and the ability to beat teams with your arm. He has both pieces, the way Michael Vick and Donovan McNabb do.

Steve McNair
Tennessee Titans quarterback

———

He'll be one of the great pro quarterbacks we've ever seen play. He'll be in the Hall of Fame.

Mack Brown
on Young

———

I think being quarterback of this team is what God put me on earth for.

Vince Young
*the only player in NCAA history to pass
for more than 230 yards and rush for more
than 250 yards in the same game
(against Oklahoma State, 2005)*

THE GREAT
TEXAS BACKS

He's the quickest football player I've ever seen. He's like a balloon full of air. When you turn him loose, there's no telling where he's going, and when the play is over, he's spent.

Darrell Royal

on James Saxton,
Longhorns halfback from 1959 through '61

In the backfield Royal had Jim Saxton, a flashy, 165-pound speedster who could run the 100-yard dash in 9.9 and was to provide Texas fans with some of the most brilliant plays in Texas football history.

Gene Schoor

An average back would have been stopped at the line. A good back might have made five yards.

Bill Meek
*former SMU head coach,
on James Saxton's 80-yard touchdown run
against the Mustangs in 1961. Saxton gained
Associated Press Back of the Week honors for
his performance, which included 173 rushing
yards in the 27–0 victory*

He runs faster than small-town gossip.

Darrell Royal
*on 1961 consensus All-America halfback
James "Jackrabbit" Saxton*

THE JACKRABBIT
IN JAMES SAXTON

For those fortunate to have seen James Saxton run the football for Texas back in the late 1950s and early '60s, all would admit it was an eye-popping visual experience. Those were the days of the "broken-field runner," as scatbacks like Saxton were labeled. The hipswiveling, juking, feinting-type running backs of that ilk—Barry Sanders is a modern example—are more and more becoming relics of the past, as great overall speed, particularly on defense, redefines today's game.

Saxton ran like a jackrabbit, and opponents never knew for sure, with his great stop-start ability, in which direction he would dart next. The "Jackrabbit" epithet came legitimately while working on a cattle ranch one summer in Kaufman, Texas. Plowing an alfalfa field one day, the Palestine native spotted a horde of jackrabbits. It looked like fun, so he jumped from the tractor and gave chase. Knowing the rabbits tended to run in a circle, Saxton cut one off at midpoint and actually caught it. A local newspaper wrote up an account of the event, and thus was born the descriptive moniker of the future Texas consensus All-America halfback.

He was sudden. It was unbelievable how he'd be here and then he'd be over there.

Darrell Royal
on the skittery moves of James "Jackrabbit" Saxton, who led the Longhorns in rushing pass receiving, punt returns, and interceptions his junior season of 1960

—◊◊◊—

James Saxton would have been a great receiver. He could start and stop so quickly, he could be at full speed in two steps. It was like he was jet-propelled.

Bobby Lackey
quarterback (1957–59)

—◊◊◊—

Jim Saxton averaged 8.3 yards per carry in 1961, had TD runs of 80, 79, 66, 56, 49, and 45 yards, and was a consensus All-American.

Gene Schoor

—◊◊◊—

Replacing James Saxton was practically impossible.

Darrell Royal

Although he was listed at 180 pounds, Chris Gilbert was an undersized 165-pounder. Much like Longhorn great James Saxton, Gilbert compensated with terrific quickness and balance.

John Maher
Kirk Bohls

~~~

He had tremendous stamina for a guy who weighs 165. Gilbert was durable and had exceptional balance. His feet were cat-like. It looked like he had an extra leg. . . . Watching Chris run is like a film strip with several frames missing—you see him hit a hole here and all of a sudden he's way over here, and you don't see how he got over there.

Darrell Royal

We were having difficulty moving the ball. Just before halftime, I was going around end, got hit, and almost turned a flip. Well, after doing the flip, I was still on my feet and went on for a 10- or 12-yard gain. That got the team perked up, and then they put me on the starting team.

Chris Gilbert
on his first game as a Longhorn, against
Southern Cal in 1966

Against Baylor in Waco, in 1966, it was the one-man wrecking crew, Chris Gilbert, who scored two touchdowns and established a Texas rushing record of 245 yards in 24 carries as the Horns defeated the Bears 26–14.

Gene Schoor

Against Arkansas in 1967, Chris Gilbert rushed for 162 yards on a school-record 38 carries to become the all-time Texas rushing leader midway through his junior season.

John Maher
Kirk Bohls

FAST FACT: The Longhorns intercepted five passes and held on for a 21–12 win behind Gilbert's three touchdowns.

—◊◊◊—

I seemed to have a gift. I think I had a knack for finding the hole, and I was fairly quick off the start. And I never missed any games.

Chris Gilbert

—◊◊◊—

He broke it open, but that run didn't impress me. Those five- and six-yard runs when it was thick was when you became a Chris Gilbert fan.

Darrell Royal
on Gilbert's phenomenal 203-yard rushing performance against TCU in 1967, which included a SWC-record 96-yard touchdown run

T he only weapon we had was Gilbert and a decent defense. If I could have been healthy enough to help Chris, he'd probably have rushed for 1,500 or 1,700 yards.

Bill Bradley
*who injured his knee during the 1966
campaign and underwent an operation
after the season*

C hris Gilbert replaced TCU's Jim Swink as the SWC's all-time leading rusher with a 213-yard day against Rice in 1968. He turned in another 200-yard perform- ance versus Baylor and was one of three Longhorns to gain more than 100 yards, the first time that had been accomplished in 16 years.

**John Maher
Kirk Bohls**

I think Gilbert was the best running back who ever played at the University. He ran a 9.6 in the 100-yard dash. He could cut on a dime. He had super moves and was durable as all get out. Earl Campbell is considered maybe the best running back who ever played, but I don't think he was the all-around running back Chris was.

Bill Bradley

He was popping open like a morning glory.

Darrell Royal

on fullback Roosevelt Leaks, after the Horns' battering ram pounded Rice for 154 yards in the first half of a 45–9 defeathering of the Owls in 1972

R osey was a tremendous runner. He was so strong he drilled it up in there and had the ability to keep people away from his legs. Earl is given a lot of credit for breaking (the racist) image we had, but Roosevelt Leaks was the first to come here and be a superstar. He attracted the Earl Campbells and the Raymond Clayborns and Alfred Jacksons.

Darrell Royal

—〰—

R osey, I think, was a little quicker getting to the line, but no one could compare with Earl's power. Earl would rather run over 'em than dodge 'em.

Marty Akins
quarterback (1973–75)

E arl was better than me, no question about it. He was bigger and faster, and he had that natural instinct.

Roosevelt Leaks

———ᴡᴡ———

T hat was the game that Earl ran into the end zone and ran into Bevo and Bevo fell down.

Randy McEachern
quarterback (1977–78),
on the Horns' 35–21 triumph over Houston
in 1977

———ᴡᴡ———

A long time ago someone said to me, "A person is not measured by the breaths he takes, but by the breathless moments he creates." And Earl has created more breathless moments than anybody I have ever been around.

Fred Akers
on Campbell

My favorite play was right in front of OU's bench in the 1977 game. I think every defender hit Earl Campbell twice on the same play. It was a seven-yard gain. And he twisted and turned and was hit and came back off of it so many times. Then the official made a mistake and thought he was down and he wasn't. He came out of it and they blew the play dead. It was a great run. Some of his very best runs were from four to 10 yards.

Fred Akers

He is one of only two three-time winners of the NFL's MVP award.

Douglas S. Looney
on Earl Campbell

The University of Texas

Earl Campbell

Ricky Williams finished his junior season with 1,893 yards rushing and was better in nearly every statistical category than Earl Campbell was when the "Tyler Rose" won the Heisman Trophy in 1977. Trouble was Williams's team finished just 4–7 and Campbell's team went unbeaten before losing to Notre Dame in the Cotton Bowl.

Steve Richardson

—〰—

Ricky reminds me so much of myself it's scary. He has those big ol' thighs that I used to have back when I was young and runs a lot like I did. I think he's faster than I was, but the way he takes on defenders and runs over them brings back a lot of memories.

Earl Campbell
*on fellow Heisman Trophy winner
Ricky Williams*

Ricky Williams

After running for 223 yards in a 27–24 win in 1997 against Oklahoma, Ricky Williams warmed hearts by wearing No. 37 in Doak Walker's memory and racing for 139 yards and two scores in a 34–3 win in the 1998 OU game.

Brian Davis
Chip Brown

—∿∿—

It hurts to tackle him. When you tackle Ricky Williams, you better have your brother, your sister, and everybody else along with you when you try to pull him down.

Bob Simmons
Oklahoma State head coach (1995–2000)

09

MAJOR MOMENTS

I t was the greatest game since the end of World War II. The greatest play of the decade was the fourth-and-three play by Street. It was the biggest thing to happen in the Southwest Conference since the Alamo.

Beano Cook
college football analyst and, in 1969, NCAA press director for ABC television, on the Big Shootout

Noble Doss, The Impossible Catch

S ure, I've worked you hard, harder than you've ever worked before, but this is the biggest game in the history of your great school. And you, all of you, will be remembered for what happens on that field today, when you beat Notre Dame.

Jack Chevigny
head coach (1934–36)

FAST FACT: Chevigny's David-vs.-Goliath Texas team of 1934 upset mighty Notre Dame 7–6 before 33,000 at Knute Rockne Stadium in South Bend. It was considered the greatest Longhorn gridiron victory to that time.

—⁘⁘⁘—

I 've accused Noble of catching that pass with his eyes shut.

Wally Scott
end (1940–42),
on The Impossible Catch—Noble Doss's
legendary over-the-shoulder reception to the
Texas A&M 1-yard line that helped upset the
previously undefeated and No. 1-ranked
Aggies in 1940

Pete Layden hurled a high, arching pass to Noble Doss. It seemed Doss would be unable to get to the ball, it was far out of his reach. But with an incredible effort Doss leaped high into the air, and with his back to his quarterback, made one of those unbelievable catches that have to be seen to be believed.

Gene Schoor

on Doss's legendary "Impossible Catch" to the Aggie 1-yard line on the third play of the game, setting up the only score in the Horns' 7–0 win over Texas A&M in 1940

BOWLING LAYNE

The legendary Bobby Layne was never better than in his two bowl appearances as the Longhorns' star quarterback. His offensive fireworks against Missouri in the 1946 Cotton Bowl rank as one of college football's all-time great individual performances.

Layne scored four touchdowns, running for three and hauling in a 50-yard bomb from Ralph Ellsworth for a fourth score. The ubiquitous UT signal-caller also kicked four extra points and tossed a pair of touchdown passes good for 48 and 25 yards. With Layne literally having a hand—or foot—in every Texas point, the Longhorns beat the Tigers, 40–27. His passing was near perfection that afternoon, with 11-of-12 aerials completed for 158 yards— the only incompletion a dropped pass.

Two New Years Days later, Texas squared off against Alabama in the 1948 Sugar Bowl, a game billed as a showdown between two of the nation's premier college quarterbacks: Alabama's Harry Gilmer and Layne. Seventy-three thousand fans witnessed Gilmer's under-achieving performance of just four completions for 31 yards, while Layne completed 10-of-24 passes for 183 yards and a 27–7 victory.

In both bowl games, Layne was named the game's outstanding player.

In Fort Worth, Texas allowed TCU to score four touchdowns for a 27–7 lead, but the Longhorns put together two exciting touchdowns in the final ten minutes of play. Then, with two minutes to play, Del Womack piled through TCU for another score. Buck Lansford kicked the extra point slightly to the right of the crossbars, but the ball veered and just hit the top of the post and fell in for the extra point. It was the margin of victory in an incredible come-from-behind 35–34 win, one of the most exciting games Texas had ever played.

Gene Schoor
on the 1954 Texas-TCU classic

That was a big victory. We ran a lot of quick-motion passes. I would have hated to have played Ole Miss a 10-game schedule, but we were good too. We were the equal of teams in the picture for the national championship.

Darrell Royal

on Texas's 12–7 victory over Mississippi in the 1962 Cotton Bowl. The win, Royal's first Cotton Bowl triumph as UT head coach, was aided by five Longhorn interceptions. Four years earlier, Royal's Horns had been trounced by Ole Miss 39–7 in the 1958 Sugar Bowl

We got them right where we want them.

Johnny Treadwell

*to fellow linebacker Pat Culpepper,
on UT's famous goal-line stand against
Arkansas in 1962. Treadwell and Culpepper
guessed right, standing up Razorback fullback
Danny Brabham on third-and-goal, causing
the Hogs' runner to fumble. Texas recovered
to preserve a 7–3 triumph*

We tried to wipe their line out to set up the runner for the linebackers. It was a big play in the history of Texas.

Johnny Treadwell

*on the above-mentioned goal-line stand
against Arkansas in '62*

I remember landing, thinking I was on the 1-yard line. It made for a dramatic finish.

Duke Carlisle

quarterback/safety (1961–63),
on his game-saving end zone interception
against Baylor to preserve a 7–0 victory and
keep Texas undefeated at 8–0 during their
national championship run in 1963

—〰—

President Kennedy was headed to Austin. Coach Royal was going to give him a football. It was incredibly sad.

Duke Carlisle

on the aftermath of the presidential
assassination in 1963. The Longhorns played
archrival Texas A&M just six days after the
horrific event. Royal was about to depart for
the Austin airport to meet the president and
hand him a football, when news of the
assassination broke

W e had to contain him at all cost. We told our ends to stay upfield and not to let him reverse his field. It was like covering a kickoff. I think he was the best scrambling passer we ever faced.

Darrell Royal

on Navy All-America quarterback and Heisman Trophy winner Roger Staubach, following Texas's decisive 28–6 victory over the Midshipmen in the 1964 Cotton Bowl, solidifying the Longhorns' first consensus national championship

I don't have any idea what Darrell Royal told his team at halftime today. But some Monday morning when I've got a hangover and don't want to get up and go to work, when I'd just as soon lie there and maybe die, I just wish he'd walk into my bedroom and tell me the same thing he told them.

Bill Van Fleet

former Fort Worth Star-Telegram *sportswriter,
following the 1967 OU-Texas game, in which
the Sooners dominated the first half but
eventually lost 9–7 to the Horns, knocking
Oklahoma out of a national title*

I t was a play up the middle. I cut to the outside, and it was just a footrace down the sidelines. I didn't know it was a record until I heard Wally Pryor say it over the PA system.

Chris Gilbert

on his SWC-record 96-yard touchdown run against TCU in 1967. Gilbert posted 203 rushing yards that day

—⁓—

T he year before, Texas A&M had intercepted four of my passes. I felt by the end of the 1968 A&M game, the tag, "Super Bill," was something I earned.

Bill Bradley

after intercepting four passes in '68 against the Aggies. Bradley went on to star with the Philadelphia Eagles for eight seasons— a three-time Pro Bowler who intercepted 34 passes for a team record (tied) that still stands

gainst SMU, Texas put on an exhibi-
tion, the likes of which had been seen
only once before and only two times since.
All four Longhorn backs rushed for more
than 100 yards, a feat first accomplished by
Arizona State in 1951 and later duplicated
only by Alabama in 1973 and Army in 1984.

John Maher
Kirk Bohls

on the 1969 backfield of fullback Steve
Worster (137), quarterback James Street (121),
and halfbacks Jim Bertelsen (137) and Ted
Koy (111) that pounded the Mustang defense
for 676 total yards, second highest in
Longhorn annals, in a 45–14 obliteration

That day the eyes of the entire nation were upon Texas.

Bill Little

*former UT sports information director
(1983–94)/author,
following the December 6, 1969,
Game of the Century vs. Arkansas*

—◊◊—

Of course, it was a perfect throw and a perfect catch. People talk about that being a brave call and a courageous call and a great call. If that pass had been incomplete, it'd been the most criticized call. . . . But we weren't moving the ball that well. So I felt we had to gamble, had to go for it. We were behind. We had to do something.

Darrell Royal

*on quarterback James Street's late-fourth-
quarter 44-yard completion to Randy Peschel
on fourth-and-3 that broke the Razorbacks'
stranglehold on Texas in the 1969 showdown
at Fayetteville*

One of the [Arkansas] defenders said that he thinks the ball grazed his fingertips as it went into Randy Peschel's hands. That's how close it was to being an unsuccessful play. And had it been unsuccessful, Lord knows they'd still be criticizing me.

Darrell Royal

on the big play of The Big Shootout: James Street's 44-yard pass to Peschel on fourth-and-3 from the Longhorns' 43-yard line. Texas scored two plays later to take a heart-stopping 15–14 win over Arkansas at Fayetteville, December 6, 1969

—∿∿—

When I first looked back, I thought, "This is overthrown." I just kept running and looked back again, and there it was.

Randy Peschel

end (1967–69), on THE play of The Big Shootout

Three guys go for the ball and, give the guy credit, he makes a miraculous catch.

Jerry Moore
*former Arkansas Razorbacks defensive back,
on Randy Peschel's legendary catch in the
1969 Texas-Arkansas classic*

Come on! It was a great call, a great throw, a great catch. How many times out of ten could they execute that? That might have been the only time. But you only need to do it once.

Terry Don Phillips
*former Arkansas defensive tackle,
on the James Street-to-Randy Peschel pass
in the Game of the Century*

We just didn't play well. Arkansas outplayed us in that football game.

Darrell Royal
on the 15–14 nail-biter at Fayetteville in '69

ORVILLE'S ODYSSEY

In the summer prior to the 1969 college football season, longtime *Arkansas Gazette* sports editor Orville Henry wrote a *Twilight Zone*-type preseason pigskin forecast for his paper. Henry's eerie prediction cites the scheduling change from October to December of the Texas-Arkansas game and the dramatic conclusion of the season's final week (read: Big Shootout).

"You're there," said Henry. "President Nixon is there. Mickey Herskowitz, maybe even Red Smith is there. Chris Schenkel and Bud Wilkinson and a 67-man ABC-TV crew are there. Hoss Cartwright is there. Everybody is there. The landscape is wintry rather than autumnal, but Razorback Stadium glows with color; red and burnt orange on all sides of the fluorescent-green AstroTurf, flags flying, balloons ascending.

"The time is at hand for the most ballyhooed kickoff in Southwest Conference history. Arkansas and Texas, 9–0 on each side of the field, are playing for the national collegiate football championship."

We were going to be hostages. It was like being the Beatles. Fans were trying to come into the plane. We finally made it off and bolted.

James Street
on the reception from more than 10,000
fans at Robert Mueller Airport welcoming the
victorious Longhorns home after the classic
Big Shootout triumph over Arkansas,
December 6, 1969

In the 1970 Cotton Bowl against Notre Dame, Texas came from behind with two and a half minutes left to play and defeated the Irish 21–17. On two occasions, Jim Street converted fourth-down plays on the drive—one at the Irish 20-yard line, the second at the Notre Dame 10.

Gene Schoor
on the victory that cemented UT's
second national championship

I saw James Street at a Mexican restaurant in Houston a couple years ago, and we laughed about the game. I still say Street is one of the luckiest people I have known in my life.

Joe Theismann

Notre Dame quarterback who directed the Irish against Texas in the 1970 Cotton Bowl, referring to Street's and the Longhorns' 21–17 comeback victory, in which Cotton Speyrer dug Street's critical late fourth quarter fourth-and–2 pass off the grass tops for an eight-yard gain to keep UT's winning drive alive

—

I t was like a fairy-tale world. You know, the way I look at it, something good's going to happen to me. I always think I'm going to get lucky.

James Street

R oosevelt Leaks rushed for a spectacular total of 342 yards, shattering the
Southwest Conference record and tying
him for third place in the NCAA's all-time
record books.

Gene Schoor

*on the bruising fullback's career day in a
42–14 Texas win against SMU in 1973*

—◊◊◊—

T hat was a tiring day. Our people were a
little bit bigger than theirs, and we
were blowing the holes open. I got to touch
the ball almost every time.

Roosevelt Leaks

*on his 342-yard rushing performance, eight
yards shy of the NCAA record, in Texas's
42–14 victory over SMU in 1973, in which
Leaks smashed A&M fullback Bob Smith's
all-time single-game SWC rushing mark
of 297 yards*

The Razorbacks were paralyzed by the brilliance of Earl Campbell's play. Texas took a 38–7 victory.

Gene Schoor

on Campbell's stunning all-around performance against Arkansas on national television in 1974, in which the Texas freshman scored one touchdown on a 68-yard run and set up two other TDs, including one on a blocked punt

I think this was the greatest win of my coaching career.

Fred Akers

on Texas's 14–12 come-from-behind victory over Alabama in the 1982 Cotton Bowl. Trailing 7–0 at the half, the Longhorns tallied two fourth-quarter touchdowns behind the quarterbacking of Bob Brewer and the running of Terry Orr for the win

I over pursued, and Bo cut back on me. I was thinking there was no way I could get him. I was running as best I could. Watching the films the next day, I remember everyone was amazed that I was able to catch him from behind. I was, too.

Jerry Gray
*defensive halfback (1981–84),
on his rundown of Auburn's future Heisman
Trophy winner Bo Jackson, saving a sure
touchdown to preserve the Longhorns' 35–27
victory over the Tigers in 1984. Jackson, who
ran the 40 in under 4.2, reeled off 53 yards
before Gray's tackle, which resulted in a
separated right shoulder for Jackson*

James Brown had taken "fourth and inches" and made it into a euphoria that will forever rank as one of the greatest moments in the storied history of Longhorn football.

Bill Little

on Brown's 61-yard pass to tight end Derek Lewis down to the Nebraska 11 with under three minutes to play and Texas holding on to a 30–27 lead over the Cornhuskers in the first-ever Big 12 championship game, at the TWA Dome in St. Louis, December 7, 1996. Running back Priest Holmes took it in shortly thereafter for his third TD of the game, and Texas went on to win 37–27

I think that was the turning point in the season.

Greg Davis

on the school-record 97-yard touchdown pass from quarterback Major Applewhite to wide receiver Wane McGarity in UT's 34–3 victory over Oklahoma in 1998. The Horns went on to win five of their remaining six games, including a 38–11 Cotton Bowl triumph over Mississippi State

N ever in the 90-year history of the Rose Bowl had a game been decided on the final play. But in year 91, on January 1, 2005, it was.

Bill Little

on UT's 2004 season-capping come-from-behind 38–37 Rose Bowl win over Michigan on kicker Dusty Mangum's 37-yard field goal

I think he's trying to win this thing by himself . . . and if we give him a little help, I think he'll do it.

Greg Davis
*on Vince Young's 2005 Rose Bowl
MVP performance, in which the Longhorns'
sophomore quarterback rang up 372 yards of
total offense, running for 192 yards and four
touchdowns and passing for 180 yards and
another TD in leading Texas to a stirring
38–37 win over Michigan*

That is a game that will be remembered forever. They'll be talking about that one long after you and I are both gone.

Darrell Royal
*to Mack Brown,
following the Longhorns' thrilling one-point
win over Michigan in the 2005 Rose Bowl*

T he most anticipated non-conference game played in Ohio Stadium in at least a decade—and maybe ever—started with flash bulbs popping and the Horseshoe-record crowd of 105,565 in a frenzy. The raucous atmosphere left the Longhorns, who have won 22 of 23 on the road, unfazed. They calmly scored on their first two drives with Vince Young running and passing like a pro.

Associated Press

on the start of the first-ever meeting between Texas and Ohio State early in the 2005 season. The Longhorns came from behind to win a thriller, 25–22

L imas Sweed came off the ball real good. I threw the ball to the outside so he could go out of bounds or make the great play, and Sweed made a great play for us.

Vince Young

on his go-ahead 24-yard TD pass that put Texas up 23–22 over Ohio State with 2:37 remaining, September 10, 2005, at Ohio Stadium, in the first-ever meeting between the two powerhouses. The Horns added a safety, winning 25–22

—⟶

I t was the worst train wreck in the dubious history of conference championship games.

Pat Forde

following UT's 70–3 rout of Colorado in the 2005 Big 12 championship game

We were into the wind, we were backed up, we were third-and-10, and what a great play, what a great run. Talk about Heisman Trophy winners. That's a highlight reel for a Heisman Trophy right there.

Mack Brown

after Vince Young's 80-yard scramble for a touchdown that ignited a Texas comeback from 19 points down in the third quarter against Oklahoma State in 2005. The run pushed UT ahead, 34–28; the Horns eventually gunned down the Cowboys, 47–28, behind Young's spectacular "200–200" game —rushing for a career-high 267 yards and passing for 239 more yards en route to setting a school record for total offense in a single game

e goin' to the 'ship!

Happy Horns

*following their 70–3 annihilation of Colorado
in the 2005 Big 12 championship game.
The win sent No. 2 Texas to the national
championship game against No. 1 USC*

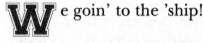

evo's going back to Beverly Hills.

Pat Forde

*after UT's 2005 Big 12 title game win
over Colorado. The victory put the Longhorns
back in the Rose Bowl for the second
consecutive year*

I had to get in there. In the heat of battle, five years in the program, I just went for it.

Michael Huff

*safety (2002–05),
on the critical stuff of USC's LenDale White
on fourth-and–2 at the Texas 45 with just 2:13
remaining in the 2005 BCS title game and
with UT still trailing 38–33. Co-defensive
coordinator Gene Chizik had called for a blitz
that did not include Huff. Huff went in
anyway, making the key stop that gave the
ball back to the Longhorns*

Vince Young's wild dash ended one of those rare Games of the Century that lived up to its billing—and then some.

Andrew Bagnato

*writer, Arizona Republic,
on the 2005 national championship game,
one of the greatest Rose Bowls ever, in which
Texas stunned No. 1-ranked USC, ending
Southern Cal's 34-game win streak and quest
for a record third straight national title. In
specific, Bagnato refers to Young's decisive
fourth-and–5 touchdown sprint of eight yards
with 19 seconds remaining to give Texas a
41–38 victory and the crown*

D o you believe Texas scored 15 points in less than four minutes? With the quarterback once panned for his throwing motion completing nine pressurized passes in the final two drives—then finally sealing the deal with the most incredible legs since Marilyn Monroe's?

Pat Forde

on the final chapter of the 2005 national championship game win over Southern Cal

THE TEXAS LONGHORNS ALL-TIME TEAM

B *obby Layne, Steve Worster, James Saxton, Chris Gilbert, Roy Williams, Michael Huff, Roosevelt Leaks, Brad Shearer, Steve McMichael—and those are just some of the players who didn't make it! The irony of every all-time team is that those not selected are often more conspicuous than those legends chosen.*

Inevitably, the task of picking such a unit becomes an exercise in creativity. For instance, one of the great offensive stars in UT history—known for his legendary Impossible Catch—makes our team at defensive back, where he still holds the top spot for career interceptions (17, tied).

Through the ages, Texas fans have been served a smorgasbord of superb athletic talent. Stand back, for this glittering array of the Burnt Orange & White's brightest requires your finest pair of shades.

THE TEXAS LONGHORNS ALL-TIME TEAM

OFFENSE	DEFENSE
Cotton Speyrer, *wide receiver*	**Tony Brackens,** *defensive end*
Hub Bechtol, *tight end*	**Scott Appleton,** *defensive tackle*
Jerry Sisemore, *tackle*	**Kenneth Sims,** *defensive tackle*
Bud McFadin, *guard*	**Bill Atessis,** *defensive end*
Bill Wyman, *center*	**Derrick Johnson,** *linebacker*
Dan Neil, *guard*	**Tommy Nobis,** *linebacker*
Bobby Wuensch, *tackle*	**Johnny Treadwell,** *linebacker*
Johnny "Lam" Jones, *wide receiver*	**Johnnie Johnson,** *defensive back*
Vince Young, *quarterback*	**Jerry Gray,** *defensive back*
Earl Campbell, *running back*	**Bobby Dillon,** *defensive back*
Ricky Williams, *running back*	**Noble Doss,** *defensive back*
Russell Erxleben, *punter/kicker*	**Eric Metcalf,** *punt returner*
	Mike Adams, *kick returner*

Darrell Royal, *coach*

COTTON SPEYRER
wide receiver (1968–70)
All-America (1969, '70), All-SWC (1969),
1969 Cotton Bowl co-Offensive MVP

I t looked like Cotton Speyrer dove eight yards. He really had to lay out to catch it. Street put it where the only person who could catch it was Speyrer. It was low and outside. And Speyrer had to stretch to get that thing. He did what was necessary to get it done.

Fred Akers

on the critical fourth-and–2 play from the Notre Dame 10-yard line with 2:26 remaining in the 1970 Cotton Bowl. James Street's successful completion to Speyrer enabled Texas to pull ahead of the Irish three plays later on Billy Dale's scoring plunge from the 1

HUB BECHTOL
Tight end (1944–46)

Consensus All-America (1945 '46),
All-SWC (1944, '45, '46),
1946 Cotton Bowl co-MVP,
College Football Hall of Fame (1991)

End Hub Bechtol closed out a remarkable career as Texas's first three-time All-American.

Gene Schoor

—◊◊◊—

Bobby Layne made me an All-American. If you're the favorite receiver of a man like that, you get a lot of passes thrown your way. He had his favorite plays, and three of our touchdown [pass] patterns went to me.

Hub Bechtol

JERRY SISEMORE
Tackle (1970–72)
Consensus All-America (1971 '72),
All-SWC (1971–72),
College Football Hall of Fame (2002)

Sisemore was a mobile monster, standing 6-foot-4 and weighing more than 250 pounds. . . . Once, in a game against SMU, press box spotter John Sobieski casually commented after a significant Longhorns running play, "Sisemore knocked down five guys on that play."

Bill Little

DAN NEIL
Guard (1993–96)
Consensus All-America (1996),
All-SWC (1995), All-Big 12 (1996)

Neil was one of the best pulling guards in UT history.

Brian Davis
Chip Brown

He built a reputation as a hard-nosed, intense competitor.

Lee Rasizer
Rocky Mountain News

BILL WYMAN

Center (1971–73)

Consensus All-America (1973),
All-SWC (1972, '73)

Bill Wyman blocked so well for tailback Roosevelt Leaks that head coach Darrell Royal would say they went together "like peanut butter and crackers."

Robert Heard
author

BUD MCFADIN

Guard (1948–50)

Consensus All-America (1950),
All-SWC (1949–50), 1951 Cotton Bowl MVP,
College Football Hall of Fame (1983)

The last thing you want to do is make that big son of a gun mad.

Pie Vann
*former Southern Mississippi head coach,
to USM lineman Pat Ferlise, scheduled to play opposite
McFadin, playing stateside for Carswell Air Force Base during
the Korean War. To test Vann's hypothesis on McFadin,
Ferlise jumped early on the game's first play, ramming a
forearm into McFadin's unfacemasked face. McFadin never
winced. That left Ferlise with just over 59 minutes to deal
with the consequences of his rash act*

BOBBY WUENSCH
Tackle (1968–70)
Consensus All-America (1970),
All-SWC (1969, '70)

A rock in the Horns' rugged O-line of the late 1960s-early '70s, Wuensch, co-captain of the UPI national championship team of 1970, opened up the right side of the Notre Dame defensive line with the block that sprang Billy Dale's winning touchdown in the 1970 Cotton Bowl to cement Texas's consensus 1969 national championship. Named to the Cotton Bowl and Southwest Conference All-Decade teams of the 1970s. The Longhorns were a combined 30–2–1 when Wuensch was in the starting lineup.

JOHNNY "LAM" JONES
Wide receiver (1976–79)
All-America (1978, '79),
All-SWC (1978, '79)

J ohnny "Lam" Jones was not just a track man. He was fast and could play football. He was a football man who could fly on the track. He was a threat as a runner. And he was aggressive; he was so tough, too. He could have been a running back and played there as a freshman [when he had 182 yards rushing against Rice]. He was not a fragile guy. He had more than just speed. He was such a beautiful athlete. He was something to see.

Fred Akers

FAST FACT: Even more to Jones's credit, he worked with six different quarterbacks during his four years at Texas.

VINCE YOUNG

Quarterback (2003–05)

Consensus All-America (2005),
Big 12 Offensive Player of the Year (2005),
All-Big 12 (2005),
2005 Maxwell Award (college football player of the year),
2005 Davey O'Brien Award (top college quarterback),
Rose Bowl MVP (2005, '06),
Big 12 Offensive Freshman of the Year (2003)

He's the finest athlete I've ever been on the field with.

Lloyd Carr
Michigan head coach

—⁓—

He makes anything he wants to happen on the football field.

Jonathan Scott
*offensive tackle (2002–05),
on Young*

EARL CAMPBELL
Running back (1974–77)

Heisman Trophy (1977),
consensus All-America (1977),
All-SWC (1974, '75, '77),
Davey O'Brien Award (1977),
NCAA rushing and scoring champion (1977),
Houston Post SWC Offensive MVP Trophy (1977),
1974 Gator Bowl MVP,
1975 Bluebonnet Bowl Offensive MVP,
College Football Hall of Fame (1990),
Pro Football Hall of Fame (1991)

He's the only player I've ever seen who could have gone right to the pros from high school.

Darrell Royal
on Earl Campbell

—〜〜—

Some of the runs he made were absolutely phenomenal. It was like he deserved to be on a different planet from the rest of us.

Johnnie Johnson
*defensive back (1976–79),
on Campbell*

RICKY WILLIAMS

Running back (1995–98)

Heisman Trophy (1998),
consensus All-America (1997 '98),
Maxwell Award (1998),
Walter Camp Football Foundation Player of the Year (1998),
Doak Walker Award (nation's top running back, 1997, '98),
NCAA rushing champion (1997, '98),
NCAA scoring champion (1998),
1999 Cotton Bowl Offensive MVP,
Big 12 Offensive Player of the Year (1997, '98),
All-Big 12 (1996, '97, '98)

He's the best player I've ever played against. I was kind of hoping he would go pro. Now, I have to put up with him again. He's phenomenal.

Dat Nguyen
*former Texas A&M and Dallas Cowboys
linebacker,
on Williams's decision to return for his
senior year at UT*

TONY BRACKENS
Defensive end (1993–95)
Consensus All-America (1995),
All-SWC (1993, '94, '95)

A lways seemed to have a big game against Oklahoma but none was bigger than in 1995, when Brackens had 12 tackles, including two sacks, and blocked a field goal in a 24–24 tie.

Brian Davis
Chip Brown

SCOTT APPLETON
Defensive tackle (1961–63)
Consensus All-America (1963),
Outland Trophy (nation's top interior lineman, 1963),
All-SWC (1962, '63)

B locking Scott Appleton was like trying to block smoke. He slipped off blocks better than anybody I ever saw.

Darrell Royal

—∼∼—

I n one of the colossal showdowns—the Sooners were No. 1 and the Horns No. 2—Appleton took over with 18 tackles and a fumble recovery as UT rolled to a 28–7 victory in 1963.

Brian Davis
Chip Brown

KENNETH SIMS

Defensive tackle (1978–81)

Consensus All-America (1980, '81),
Lombardi Trophy (nation's top lineman, 1981),
All-SWC (1980, '81),
Houston Post 1981 SWC MVP Trophy (defense)

I think Kenneth Sims was the best defensive tackle that we ever had. Kenneth would have to be listed among the great defensive linemen of college football any year. He would be one of those all-timers. You didn't have to make a highlight film of his plays. Just put a game film out there.

Fred Akers

BILL ATESSIS

Defensive end (1968–70)

Consensus All-America (1970),
All SWC (1969, '70)

Two-hundred-fifty-pound Bill Atessis charged from his left end slot and moved the entire right side of the OU line back one yard.

Robert Heard
during UT's 41–9 romp over the Sooners in 1970

DERRICK JOHNSON
Linebacker (2001–04)

Consensus All-America (2003, '04),
2004 Butkus Award (nation's top college linebacker),
Nagurski Award (nation's outstanding defensive
player, 2004), All-Big 12 (2002, '03, '04),
Big 12 Defensive Freshman of the Year (2001),
2001 Holiday Bowl Defensive MVP

Derrick Johnson is as good a linebacker as anybody that we have played against in our history. He is a big playmaker. . . . Even when we blocked him, he just defeated us. Personally that hurt us big time, he was that kind of dominating player.

Ken Hatfield
former Rice head coach

—⧟⧟—

I'm like a heat-seeking missile, and the ball carrier is my target.

Derrick Johnson

TOMMY NOBIS
Linebacker (1963–65)

Consensus All-America (1965),
Maxwell Award (1965), Outland Trophy (1965),
All-SWC (1963, '64, '65),
Houston Post 1964 SWC MVP Trophy (defense),
College Football Hall of Fame (1981)

Tommy Nobis is the best linebacker I've ever seen in college football.

Paul Dietzel
*former head coach at LSU, Army,
and South Carolina*

━━∿━━

Tommy Nobis is a once-in-a-lifetime player. He's a perfect type of a kid. One player like Nobis can make the difference between a winning team and a losing one.

Hayden Fry
*former head coach at SMU,
North Texas State, and Iowa*

JOHNNY TREADWELL
Linebacker (1960–62)
Consensus All-America (1962),
All-SWC (1962), Academic All-America (1961, '62),
Houston Post 1962 SWC MVP Trophy (defense)

You didn't want to walk by Johnny Treadwell on Thursday or later because he was liable to forearm you.

Tommy Nobis
*linebacker (1963–65),
on his predecessor at linebacker, notorious for
his game face*

JOHNNIE JOHNSON
Defensive back (1976–79)
Consensus All-America (1978, '79),
All-SWC (1977 ,'78 ,'79)

He was one of those guys who got some votes for the Heisman. He was just outstanding at every level. He didn't just line up and make those interceptions and tackles. He was a heck of a punt returner. This guy had courage few have. And he was very, very coachable and a good leader. He could play corner and safety.

Fred Akers
on Johnson

JERRY GRAY
Defensive back (1981–84)
Consensus All-America (1983–84), All-SWC (1983–84)

Jerry Gray was like Johnnie Johnson. He was in the same category. Jerry was like another coach out there on the field. He was just a tremendously talented player. He played cornerback as well as safety. He wanted to know everything about it.

Fred Akers

BOBBY DILLON
Defensive back (1949–51)
All-America (1951), All-SWC (1951)

All-America safety Bobby Dillon went on to star for the Green Bay Packers for eight seasons and made All-Pro five years in a row, from 1954 to 1958.

**John Maher
Kirk Bohls**

—∽—

That Dillon sure is a handy man, isn't he?

Blair Cherry
on the Texas safety, who returned a punt 84 yards for a touchdown and made a game-saving interception in Texas's 27–20 win over Baylor in 1950

NOBLE DOSS
Defensive back (1939–41)

With deference to great Texas secondary men Mossy Cade, Stanley Richard, Lance Gunn, Bryant Westbrook, Quentin Jammer, Nathan Vasher, Rod Babers, and Michael Huff, Doss—remembered primarily in Horns history for his "Impossible Catch" in UT's 7–0 win over Texas A&M in 1940—was a two-way star who just happens to still hold a venerable school mark: most career interceptions, 17 (tied by Vasher in 2003). Quite a feat, in light of today's stepped-up passing game and the fact that Doss was required to play a full 60-minute game.

RUSSELL ERXLEBEN
Punter/placekicker (1975–78)
All-America (1976 '77, '78), All-SWC (1976, '77, '78)

He was not just a great kicker; he was a great punter. He could hit 67-yard field goals or 67-yard punts. When you have a guy like that, everybody knows about him.

Fred Akers

—∽∿∿—

Erxleben had nine punts and two field goals in a 6–6 tie against Oklahoma in 1976. In a 13–6 victory in 1977, he kicked field goals of 64 and 58 yards and had punts of 71 and 69 among his nine.

Brian Davis
Chip Brown

ERIC METCALF
Punt returner (1985–88)
All-SWC (1986, '87, '88)

Eric Metcalf, who could stop and start like a hummingbird, flashed some incredible moves in his Texas career.

John Maher
Kirk Bohls

—◊◊◊—

Eric Metcalf, the speedy halfback whose father set rushing records in the NFL for the St. Louis Cardinals in the 1970s, rushed for a 200-yard game and scored twice against TCU in 1987, as the Horns won that battle, 24–21. The following week, against Baylor, Metcalf gained 165 yards and a touchdown as the Horns won, 34–16.

Gene Schoor

MIKE ADAMS
Kick returner (1992–93, 1995–96)
All-SWC (1993, '95)

R oy Williams and I wanted to come in and leave a legacy. We looked up to Mike Adams. If we keep going the way we have been, we'll be up there with him.

B. J. Johnson
wide receiver (2000–03)

FAST FACT: *Adams, in addition to holding UT game/ season/career records for kickoff return yards, also was a standout wide receiver, once holding Texas career marks for most receptions, yards, and touchdown catches—all eclipsed by Williams by the end of 2003.*

DARRELL ROYAL
Head coach (1957–76)

Consensus national championships (1963, '69),
UPI national championship (1970),
SWC championships (1959, '61, '63, '68,'69,'70,'71, '72, '73, '75),
ABC-TV 1960s Coach of the Decade,
Football Writers Assn. of America Coach of the Year (1963,'69,'70),
Texas Sports Hall of Fame (1976),
Oklahoma Sports Hall of Fame (1992),
Cotton Bowl Hall of Fame (1998),
College Football Hall of Fame (1983)

Coach Royal is a Texas treasure. He taught us how to win with class and how to get back to work when we lost.

Pat Culpepper

You are the finest example of an inspiring and worthy leader I know.

Lyndon B. Johnson
on Darrell Royal

THE GREAT
TEXAS TEAMS

You think about all the great teams that came before us, just to be mentioned with them is an honor.

Frank Okam
defensive tackle (2004–)
on the 2005 Steers

I would put that 1941 team close to the top of the list. They could have beaten anybody they played. I think that team is what turned the football program completely around. Up until 1941, nobody was afraid to play the University of Texas. From then on to the present day, they made people recognize the football team at the University of Texas.

Rooster Andrews

—✍—

Arguably the best team in the first half century of Texas football was the 1941 team. Orban "Spec" Sanders was a reserve halfback on that team, and he was the sixth player picked in the NFL Draft—chosen ahead of any of the players on that great team.

Bill Little

T hat '42 team had some tough cookies. We played mean football.

Wally Scott
end (1941–42)

—◊◊◊—

O ur '42 team is the third-ranked defensive team in NCAA records. We all lined up toe to toe. There were no spreads or nothing. Then Mr. Bible split me out six inches. He thought that was big stuff.

Wally Scott

> *FAST FACT: Scott maintains that only Fordham's famed "Seven Blocks of Granite"—with Alex Wojciechowicz and Vince Lombardi—and Texas A&M's 1939 team were better defensive teams.*

—◊◊◊—

S eventy years after Texas's first football game, the Longhorns were the best team in the nation.

Gene Schoor
on the 1963 national championship team

That '61 team had more darters. This one has more power.

Frank Broyles
on the 1963 national champion
Texas Longhorns

—◊◊◊—

I think that's the best defensive team I've ever played against. I was really just beaten on. I was sorer after that game than any game I ever played in....They had Jim Hudson, Tommy Nobis, and Scott Appleton. It's really a bitter disappointment. But we got beat by a great Texas team.

Roger Staubach
on the 1963 Longhorns,
following No. 2 Navy's 28–6 loss to Texas
in the 1964 Cotton Bowl

—◊◊◊—

Our '64 team was good. We should have won two national championships in a row.

Tommy Nobis

We were absolutely blowing everybody out. Defenses had no idea how to stop it. If we had wanted to run up the scores, they would have been off the charts.

Chris Gilbert
on the Wishbone-driven 1968 Steers

—◊◊◊—

Texas is the greatest football team that I've ever seen and probably will see.

Hayden Fry
*SMU head coach,
on the 1969 Texas Longhorns, following their
resounding performance against Fry's
Mustangs, whom UT poked for 676 total
yards in a 45–14 win*

—◊◊◊—

I don't think any of us knew they were as good as they were.

Dave Elmendorf
*Texas A&M 1970 consensus
All-America safety,
on the 1969 Horns*

The '63 class was strong, but it wasn't as dominating. I really don't think there's been a better group. The Worster bunch was the backbone of those three great years.

Bill Zapalac
linebacker (1968–70)

There was a tremendous amount of players on that team. I don't know if the 1969 and 1970 national championship teams were any more talented than the team we had in '77.

Alfred Jackson
wide receiver (1974–77)

We were soaking in our 11–0 season too much. We felt like we were unbeatable.

Alfred Jackson
on the top-ranked 1977 Texas team that went undefeated in the regular season, only to lose, 38–10, to Notre Dame in the Cotton Bowl

I feel like I've been stampeded by a herd of cows.

Bo Jackson
Auburn's 1985 Heisman Trophy-winning running back,
on the '83 Longhorns, after the Plainsmen's 20–7 season-opening loss. Texas held Jackson to 35 yards on seven carries

---

Texas is awesome. There's some discrepancy about who's the best team in Texas—the Cowboys or the Longhorns. Asking their offensive linemen to make two yards is like asking a tank to crush a peanut. And in all my years of coaching, this is the best defensive team I've ever seen.

Lou Holtz
former Arkansas head coach,
on the 1983 Longhorns, who crushed Holtz's Razorbacks, 31–3, en route to an 11–1 season

We had the best defense I've ever seen in college. The second best was the Oklahoma defense with the Selmon brothers. We had experience. We had speed. We had people who could dominate.

Fred Akers

on the '83 Steers that featured Jeff Leiding, Mossy Cade, and Jerry Gray, among others

We have a chance to be special.

Mack Brown

after the big 45–12 win over Oklahoma in 2005, his first victory in the Red River Rivalry as Texas head coach. Brown's 5–0 Steers would indeed be special, going on to attain their third consensus national championship

This is the best Texas team I have played.

Mike Leach

Texas Tech head coach, on the 2005 Longhorns

I f you cannot have your best game and still score 52 points, it just shows you have a chance to be really special. That just shows you the standard this team is trying to play to.

Mack Brown

*on his 2005 national champion Longhorns,
following Texas's convincing 52–17 victory over
a top-10 Texas Tech team, after falling behind
at home (7–3, first quarter) for the first time
that season*

———〰———

T he message is we are one of the top two teams in the country. We won by 62, and that's without running it up. We have to enjoy this ride, enjoy this moment.

Mack Brown

*following the 2005 Horns' 62–0 obliteration
of Baylor to go 9–0 on the season*

I don't think I've ever been on a field where I have seen so many big, strong, fast, talented kids.

Mark Mangino
Kansas Jayhawks head coach,
on the 2005 national champions,
who slaughtered KU, 66–14

—⁓—

I 've lined up on the other side against them 43 times now, and I've never seen another Texas team this good. I think in today's football they are about as good as I've seen. . . . When you put that quarterback in there, it's like putting the cherry on top of the sundae.

Merv Johnson
Oklahoma director of football operations,
on the 2005 Longhorns and QB Vince Young

There are no weaknesses on this football team. You go position-by-position with them, and they are strong across the board. It's very difficult to find any place where they fall off.

Dennis Franchione
Texas A&M coach,
on Texas's 2005 national champions

——∿——

It's a great honor [to be compared to previous Texas championship teams]. I wasn't even around at that time (1960s). My parents were barely born. We're just trying to keep that Texas tradition alive.

Tim Crowder
defensive end (2003–06),
on the 2005 national champion Longhorns

This [2005] Texas team is all about chemistry and leadership, and you can tell it.

Grant Teaff
former Baylor coach

—∽∾—

From the second half of the Oklahoma State game through halftime of the Kansas game—a three-game period—the Longhorns posted eight straight scoreless quarters. During that period, Texas outscored its opponents 152–0.

Tim Griffin
on the 2005 Longhorns

12

THE GREAT RIVALRIES

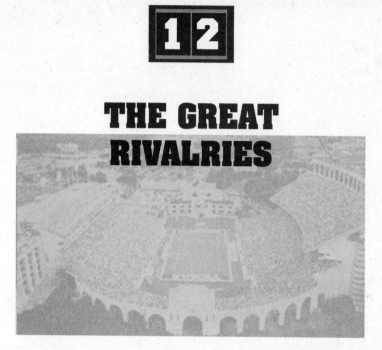

If Yale vs. Harvard can best be described as an intellectual rivalry, the Texas-Oklahoma game is just the opposite. It is raw, rugged, and deadly serious. At the moment of the kickoff, the players are jumping up and down as if they've swallowed something from the chemistry lab.

Dan Jenkins
writer, Sports Illustrated, *September 9, 1968*

B ohn Hilliard pulled in Bob Dunlap's good punt on his own 6-yard stripe and started traveling south. He picked up steam as he reached his own 30-yard mark unaided. . . . Hilliard reached the clear at midfield and from that point on the Sooners were merely taking running exercise in their own tracks in comparison with this speed merchant who left them talking to themselves as he completed his 94-yard sprint.

George White

*Dallas Morning News,
on Hilliard's record return against Oklahoma
in 1932, the longest in OU-Texas history to
that time—a mark that would last 14 years.
In this game, Hilliard accounted for 363 total
purpose yards in the 17–10 Longhorns win,
including seven punt returns for 202 yards*

We have to tone things down a bit before the OU game to make sure the band doesn't play itself out before kick-off. That game is a war to everyone involved. Not only do UT fans want to beat the Sooners, but they want to be able to say their band is better, too.

Glenn Richter
former director, Longhorn Band

—◊◊◊—

In the 1939 Texas-OU game, two-time All-American Jack Crain scored on runs of 69 and 72 yards. In 1940 his fourth-quarter touchdown beat the Sooners 19–16, and in 1941 Crain added two more touchdowns in a 40–7 runaway. In all, he scored 34 points against Oklahoma—still a series record—with five touchdowns and four conversions.

Bill Cromartie
author

Bobby Layne faded to pass and cocked his arm. Behind him circled James Canady, who took the ball from Layne's hand and skirted wide to the left for a touchdown. Texas had successfully pulled the "Statue of Liberty" play, and the Longhorn faithful howled with delight over "the oldest trick in football."

Bill Cromartie

on the 10-yard fourth-quarter touchdown climaxing UT's 20–13 win over Oklahoma in 1946

—⟪⟫—

The only way anybody's going to beat Oklahoma is to go out there and whip 'em jaw to jaw. They get a yellow dog running downhill and they'll strap him real good. The thing I want to see is that they earn what they get with some bumps and bruises.

Darrell Royal

Against an outstanding Oklahoma team in 1946, Bobby Layne and company pulled out a 20–13 win in a game that saw halfback Darrell Royal of Oklahoma almost pull victory from the jaws of defeat with several splashy runs that put the Sooners in scoring range a number of times....It was the Longhorns' seventh straight win over Oklahoma.

Gene Schoor

One year some Oklahoma fans used gasoline to burn the score in my yard. I had to take the Texas stickers off my car because someone was slashing my tires.

Jerry Scarbrough
publisher, True Orange

LACKEY NOT LACKING
AGAINST OU IN '58

It was a drought as deflating to Texans as the suffocating Dust Bowl days that had ravaged the American Southwest during the Depression: the Longhorns had lost nine of their previous ten meetings with Oklahoma, including the last six in a row. But in 1958, led by quarterback/defensive back Bobby Lackey, Texas broke the curse against the No. 2-ranked Sooners and secured one of the most revered wins in UT history.

Lackey led the Longhorns onto the scoreboard first with a 10-yard scoring pass to Rene Ramirez, then converted a two-point play to take an 8–0 lead. But the Sooners fought back to carry a 14–8 advantage with 12:52 to play. Texas, held without a first down in the second half, began a drive from its own 26 with 6:50 remaining that ended with Lackey's 7-yard TD toss to Bobby Bryant. Lackey then calmly kicked the deciding extra point with 3:10 to go to give Texas a 15–14 lead.

But it wasn't over. Lackey's great open-field tackle of Oklahoma quarterback Bobby Boyd in the final minute of play saved a possible winning score for OU. Finally, Lackey intercepted a Sooner pass at the Oklahoma 28 to preserve the win for Texas.

Texans everywhere were going absolutely mad. Possibly, the biggest upset in series history had been posted. Texas 15, Oklahoma 14.

Bill Cromartie

*on "The Bobby Lackey Game" in 1958,
in which the Longhorns' star threw a TD
pass, kicked the winning conversion, and
made a sensational open-field tackle followed
by a one-handed, game-saving interception*

—⟶⟶—

The Oklahoma era is over. It came to an end at 4:30 p.m., when the timer's gun echoed across the Cotton Bowl and University of Texas partisans erupted in a wave of celebration.

Bill Rives

*Dallas Morning News,
after the Longhorns' 19–12 win over OU
in 1959, only the third win for Texas in the
previous 12 games against Oklahoma.*

J ohnny Treadwell tried to explain how easy it is to lose your temper when you're playing for Texas against Oklahoma, but finally gave up on grounds that Webster hasn't produced enough words yet to describe the situation adequately.

Jimmy Banks

Dallas Morning News,
in the aftermath of Texas's 9–6 win over the
Joe Don Looney-led Sooners in 1962

O klahoma tried to intimidate you. If you made a tackle on them, they got up and wanted to know your name so they could get you back later.

Bobby Lackey

When you're down on the field for the OU game, it's one of the most intense feelings you can imagine. As we stand there with the flag, OU fans cuss us out and throw things at us. Even the OU band will flip us off and cuss at us as they come out of the tunnel. There really is a genuine hatred between the two schools. You literally shake with anger at some of the things their fans do, and yet you still look forward to that game more than any other.

Robert Townsend
1993 UT grad

―ᨓ―

Beating OU is like winning a national championship.

Bubba Jacques
safety (1988–91)

There may never be a defensive performance as dominating in the Texas-OU series as Tommy Nobis's 21 tackles in a 28–7 victory in 1964.

Brian Davis
Chip Brown

—◊◊◊—

It doesn't matter if they're No. 1 in the nation or No. 40. It's not hard to be up for the Okies.

Scott Appleton

—◊◊◊—

I'll never forgive God if He makes me sit out this game.

Steve Hall
tight end (1977–80),
on the prospect of missing the OU-Texas tilt
his senior season because of a broken bone on
his ring finger. Hall played.

I t was one of the greatest comebacks the University of Texas has ever had.

Fred Akers

on the 1980 Oklahoma game. Down 13–10 with under 10 minutes to play, Longhorns quarterback Donnie Little ignited a Texas charge that produced two scoring drives and a 20–13 win, with Little running for 63 of his 110 total rushing yards on those final two drives

T ake four of these and call me in the morning!

Lance Gunn

*safety (1989–92),
to Sooner fans after his fourth straight win against Oklahoma, 34–24 in 1992*

M y other records will be broken. But this is how I hope to be remembered.

Pete Gardere

quarterback (1989–92)

FAST FACT: Gardere exited Texas with virtually every significant passing mark in tow, but his flawless 4–0 mark as a starting QB against Oklahoma is unmatched in Texas annals.

Y ou got the feeling Mack Brown would rather kiss a member of the Texas A&M corps of cadets than admit how good it felt—for him, personally, not the Texas fans or the players or Bevo—to beat the snot out of Oklahoma 45–12.

Associated Press
*on the outcome of the 2005 meeting between
Texas and Oklahoma, after Brown had lost
five straight to the Sooners*

—∿∿—

J ohnnie Johnson recovered a fumble and had seven tackles in the Long- horns' 13–6 victory in 1977. He stopped OU quarterback Thomas Lott for no gain on fourth-and–1 at the Texas 5 with 4:10 remaining.

**Brian Davis
Chip Brown**

You think the same thing every year as you come down the runway. Everybody has experienced it, as a coach and as a player. There was a little tingly bubbly feeling. I felt light-headed. It felt like my feet were hardly touching the ramp; my mouth tasted like cotton.

Darrell Royal
on pregame butterflies before the
Texas-Oklahoma encounters

—〰—

UT quarterback Chris Simms failed to beat OU during his career when he was intercepted three times, sacked four times and failed to throw a touchdown pass.

Steve Richardson

—〰—

Why that's just like somebody from the United States playing for Nazi Germany.

Harold Philipp
fullback (1962–64),
on native Texans playing for Oklahoma

W hen I first came here, our three big ball games were with Oklahoma, Texas A&M, and Rice. Arkansas wasn't that big a ball game. The Texas-Arkansas game became big after Frank Broyles came to Arkansas and started being really competitive.

Darrell Royal

F rank Broyles and I never had an argument. We never had a disagreement, and we're still good friends today and still vacation together. That's when football is fun, when you have that kind of rapport with the people whom you're competing against.

Darrell Royal

The Texas-Arkansas rivalry didn't hit its zenith until the Darrell Royal-Frank Broyles coaching matchups starting in 1958. During those 19 years, 10 games decided which of the two teams would represent the Southwest Conference in the Cotton Bowl. On 11 occasions, both teams were ranked in the top 20 entering the game. And six times both were in the top 10.

Steve Richardson

It seemed like half the guys on our team were Texans, refused by Texas. So we went to Arkansas to do one thing—kick their ass. We had total respect for Darrell Royal, but we had complete respect for Frank Broyles and what he had done.

Mike Kelson
former Razorback tackle

After the 29–12 win over Arkansas in 1976, both Royal and Razorbacks head coach Frank Broyles announced their retirement from coaching. The two coaches met 20 times, with Royal's Long-horns winning 15. Royal departed as the winningest coach in the history of the now-defunct Southwest Conference.

John Wheat
author/lecturer/archivist

The Farmers, as Texas A&M was then called, had just begun to play football. . . . Texas was their first college opponent in 1894. This rivalry was to become one of the greatest, most colorful, and dramatic football series in college football. . . . Texas ran through the A&M defense almost at will, scoring eight touchdowns on the way to a 38–0 victory in Austin, establishing a rivalry that endures to this very day.

Gene Schoor

O nce you become a Longhorn you learn to hate the Aggies. A&M just brings out all these negative emotions that you never knew existed inside you.

Troy Riemer
offensive lineman (1991–93

—∽—

T he highly successful Berry M. Whitaker was gone from the head football coach's spot within two days of the A&M loss in 1922. The message was clear for future UT coaches: You don't lose to A&M in Austin and come back to coach again the next year. For the next 60 years, that maxim held true.

W. K. Stratton

Playing Texas A&M is like opening a box of Crackerjacks—there's a surprise in every package.

Darrell Royal

—◊◊◊—

Everyone wants to get their hands on my car. I've had my share of run-ins with Aggie fans over the years. One time they managed to get into my garage and paint the car maroon. Another time they tried to steal it, but being Aggies, they headed straight for College Station and got caught.

Mel Stekoll
Longhorn superfan and owner of the 1931 "Hook 'Em Horns" Chevrolet that escorts UT cheerleaders onto the field at Royal-Memorial Stadium before home games

B ack in [the mid-1960s], it was drilled into you that you did not lose to Texas A&M. You did not want to be known as the team that lost to them. If you were 10–0 and then lost to A&M, you'd be known as the team that lost to A&M.

Jim Helms

who went 4–0 against the Aggies in his four years at Texas. Helms's claim to Longhorn fame was in scoring two of the three Texas touchdowns that beat A&M in 1965, after the Steers were down 17–0 at halftime. That's the legendary game that Darrell Royal wrote "21–17" on the locker room blackboard at the half (see page 213)

I t's the most healthy rivalry I've ever been around. There's a lot of anger in the Texas-Oklahoma rivalry, and I've been on both sides of that one.

Mack Brown

on the Texas-Texas A&M rivalry. As far as being on "both sides" of the OU-UT annual war, Brown served as Oklahoma offensive coordinator in 1984 under Barry Switzer

—∾—

T his is what college football is all about. Two teams that hate each other.

Shane Dronett

defensive end/tackle (1989–91), on the Texas-Texas A&M rivalry

WINNING AND LOSING

Fellas, it's just a matter of whether we want to win or not. Now, look at these numbers. That's what this team can do. Now go on out there and win.

Darrell Royal

to his team at halftime of the 1965 game against Texas A&M, in which the Horns trailed, 17–0. Royal wrote the numbers "21–17" on the blackboard. At game's end, the final score read: Texas 21, A&M 17

There are a lot of positives in the game of football, and I always believed that in some way we could use those to help folks understand the game of life a little better.

Darrell Royal

—✺—

Following that loss to Oklahoma in 1949, a two-touchdown win over Arkansas failed to soothe my unhappy constituents. We got no credit for coming from behind in the last quarter to win. Instead we were blamed for playing such a close game.

Blair Cherry

—✺—

When we were ahead, Royal would nearly always get a blade of grass to chew on. . . . His pacing wasn't nearly as fast as when we were losing.

Gary Shaw

A letter from a well-known attorney ranted about my use of Paul Campbell at quarterback. When I told him that it wasn't easy to replace an All-American like Bobby Layne with an inexperienced youngster, he said, "I never thought Layne was so hot either."

Blair Cherry

It's harder to maintain than it is to climb. Climbing is a thrill. Maintaining is a bitch.

Darrell Royal

---

e beat the tough teams, but got beat by the weaker ones.

Ed Price
*head coach (1950–56),
on the 1951 Horns*

In the opening game of the 1953 season at LSU, Texas was upset 20–7. It was only the second season-opening loss in the 62 years that Texas had played football.

Gene Schoor

You never heard of a history teacher getting fired, even in the South, because Robert E. Lee didn't win at Appomattox.

Blair Cherry
on the perils of life on the short end

———

You hit rock bottom when you lose to the Aggies. There is no worse feeling in the world. It takes me a whole week to get over it. The thing that makes it worse than losing to OU is that you don't see OU fans until the next year. You see them stupid Aggies all over the place, and that makes you relive the whole nightmare over and over again.

Mel Stekoll

Y ou can't force people to do things. That's one of the main tricks in coaching. You have to make people want to do things because they want to win.

Darrell Royal

—ᴍ—

T hat was the worst loss Darrell Royal ever had. He said that made us put our clubs away and get our feet off the desk.

Jones Ramsey
*following the gut-wrenching 6–0 loss to TCU
in 1961. In that game, Texas All-America
halfback James Saxton was knocked out of
the contest on the game's fifth play*

We had held Arkansas to zero first downs that second half. But Jon Brittenum took them on an 80-yard drive. That really took the starch out of us. That loss may have affected me more than the one to TCU in 1961.

Darrell Royal
on the 27–24 loss to the Razorbacks in 1965

—————

This game ranks right up there with the worst.

Lawrence Sampleton
tight end (1978–81),
on the 20–6 upset loss to SMU in 1980, in
which Texas receivers dropped 11 passes and
failed to score a touchdown for the first time
in Fred Akers's tenure as UT head coach

I feel like a dog just got run over after I've had it for 12 years.

Jeff Leiding
linebacker (1980–83),
on the 28–22 loss to OU in 1982, the
Sooners' first victory in the series since 1978

—⁓—

We dominated the whole game. They might as well have dropped a nuclear warhead.

Jeff Leiding
on the Horns' loss of a national championship
in 1983 by a single point: the 10–9 Cotton Bowl
defeat by Georgia

—⁓—

That is the toughest loss we had.

Fred Akers
on the one-point 1984 Cotton Bowl loss
to Georgia

I was involved in losses before then, but I've never had a game that affected me like that. It was almost like it was some kind of mystic understanding. Nothing had to be said. Everybody packed their bags and left the locker room. It just blew up in our face.

Jeff Ward

*on the devastating 10–9 loss to Georgia
in the 1984 Cotton Bowl. With the defeat, the
Horns lost a certain national championship*

S lippery Rock could have beaten us with all the turnovers we had.

Tony Degrate

*defensive tackle (1982–84),
on the 29–15 loss to Houston in 1984,
propelled by the Cougars' five interceptions
and nine total turnovers by Texas*

It got so that winning wasn't exciting and losing became intolerable. When I first came here at age thirty-two, we'd have a win, and, man, I was so high and so happy and just thrilled beyond words. At the last, when we'd win a ball game it was just, boy, I'm glad that's over—we didn't lose. I didn't have the same thrill.

Darrell Royal

hen it works, you look smarter than taking a knee.

Mack Brown

on his go-for-it tactic with 55 seconds left in the first half of the 2005 Oklahoma game, with the Longhorns leading, 17–6. Instead of playing it conservatively, Brown pulled out the stops. QB Vince Young arched a 64-yard scoring aerial to sophomore Billy Pittman that put away the Sooners

—⁂—

I don't care if I have to run 100 times or pass it 100 times. Whatever it takes to win is all that matters to me.

Vince Young

—⁂—

I know it sounds cliché, but the guy's will is incredible. He comes through. He won't let us lose.

Justin Blalock

on quarterback Vince Young

HOOK 'EM HORNS

As a member of the Hellraisers, you can't feel self-conscious during the games. You have to be willing to do whatever it takes to keep the other fans involved. We scream and yell at every opportunity. It's not easy to stay up for an entire game, but we do it. If you don't leave exhausted, you're not doing your job.

Bradley Roberts

former vice president of the Longhorn Hellraisers, a UT student fan organization formed in 1987

People all over the world have heard of Texas because the people here are so fiercely proud of their identity.

John Mackovic
head coach (1992–97)

—〰—

No matter where you are, the fans have a bond with you and you with them. They are very proud of this bond and of their relationship with The University of Texas—and they are until Gabriel blows his horn.

John Mackovic

—〰—

Texas football is a rhythm. It's up and down. But that's what makes the ride as much fun as the winning. What we do is thrill to the University of Texas.

Bill Sansing
fan

I'm at that stage of my life where I'm much happier being a fan than a coach.

Darrell Royal

—◊—

Football is part of your upbringing in this area. By the time a kid is five, he's probably begging to play football somewhere, and he definitely expects to go to all the games.

Rooster Andrews

—◊—

UT fans don't just want the best team. They want the best band in the country, too.

Glenn Richter

—◊—

When the crowd roars, it's almost like a plane going overhead. Then there are times when the fans decide to take it up a notch. You can feel the electricity, you're flying, and you feel like you can do no wrong.

Troy Riemer

You see all these people with cowboy hats. At schools in other parts of the country, you wouldn't be caught dead wearing one. But here it's all part of the atmosphere. . . . Longhorn football is a lifestyle.

Amy Morgan
former UT cheerleader

———

If you're going to act nuts all game long, you might as well look the part.

Bradley Roberts
on face painting

———

Some fans would have us play "Texas Fight" nonstop from the kickoff right up until the end of the game. We get letters all the time telling us to do just that.

Glenn Richter

Wheeling Big Bertha, the world's largest bass drum, onto the field is no easy task. Bertha weighs 500 pounds and measures eight feet in diameter and four and a half feet in width.

Douglas S. Looney

When that music starts and the crowd gets all worked up, you have to be in a coma not to feel that rush of adrenalin.

Jimmy Saxton

My glasses have become sort of a trademark. They're painted orange and white, just like my house and a few of the rooms inside.

Mel Stekoll

You laugh, you cry, you scream and yell. And that's all before the kickoff.

Jeff Aldis
1992 UT graduate

When the fans are not supporting you, the players give up on the fans, too.

Fred Akers

You know, to this day, I still can't stand that "Hook 'Em Horns."

Joe Theismann

We wanted them to feel everything we were feeling. It was a great moment for all of us.

Vince Young

slapping hands and cheering along with Texas fans in the Cotton Bowl, in the wake of the Longhorns' monumental 45–12 victory over Oklahoma in 2005

15

THE LOCKER ROOM

I often thought we won at Texas in spite of ourselves, and consequently, the only enjoyment came immediately after a game was over, since the next day you would feel the pressure to win the upcoming game.

George Sauer
wide receiver (1963–64)

A lot of folks have questioned, since I first started running with him, why I would run with Willie Nelson. You know, they seemed to think, I guess, that a football coach at Texas is not supposed to do that, and I always gave 'em the answer. I said, "One of the reasons I like Willie is he forgives me of all my faults. And still likes me." And boy, that just spins their heads big-time.

Darrell Royal

A slim, well-built, six-foot, 170-pound freshman entered Texas on a baseball scholarship in 1944 and when he got his chance to pitch for the Texas baseball team, he was nothing short of sensational. He won game after game. In fact, he never lost a game in the Southwest Conference in his four years at Texas. Utilizing a tantalizing curve ball and marvelous control, the kid established an SWC record, winning 28 games and losing none.

Gene Schoor
on two-sport star Bobby Layne

J ust being there with those great guys was one of the great experiences of my life. I enjoyed playing baseball, but not like I came to love football. Dana Bible was like a father to me. And it was exciting when Blair Cherry took over and switched us from the single wing to the T-formation. Those were wonderful years.

Bobby Layne
quarterback (1944–47)

—〰—

W e didn't talk to each other during the game, but afterward we were telling each other how well we had done.

Doak Walker
following the 1945 Texas-SMU battle won by UT, 12–7. Walker scored the Mustangs' only TD on a 30-yard run, while his longtime pal, Longhorns quarterback Bobby Layne, hurled two touchdown passes and picked off one of Walker's passes

BE LIKE RICKY

Midland (Texas) Lee schoolboy legend Cedric Benson became one of the most highly anticipated recruits ever at the University of Texas. He was the first high school athlete to grace the cover (solo) of Dave Campbell's *Texas Football* magazine and was a four-year starter for the Longhorns. Benson capped his career in Austin by being named the 2004 Doak Walker Award winner as the nation's top running back.

Benson ran nearly step for step with UT's greatest running back of all time, Ricky Williams, finishing with 5,540 rushing yards—second only to Ricky's school-record 6,279 yards. In touchdowns scored, Benson rang up the monstrous total of 64 six-pointers, again second only to Williams's UT-record 72. His impressive 113.1 rushing yards per game average, yup, second to Ricky's walloping 136.5 average, another Texas career mark.

The similarities didn't end there. The two were roughly of the same size and build, and both sported dreadlocks during their Longhorn careers. But after Williams created negative headlines for several off-field controversies, Benson began distancing himself from the 1998 Heisman Trophy winner, the better to educate NFL scouts that the two Texas nonpareil running backs were not joined at the hip; that he, Benson, was *not* Ricky Williams. One quick snip created the desired separation.

Benson dumped the dreads.

Visualization is important for any player, but it's particularly effective for a kicker. At halftime, I don't really need to hear what the coaches have to say. I just grab my Gatorade and find a quiet area. I don't really interact with any other players. I go over every step of every kick. I'd like to tell you I'm sitting there imagining the game-winning kick, but my mind doesn't work that way. In fact, I'm probably sitting there praying I don't have to leave the sidelines during the last few minutes of the game.

Scott Szeredy
placekicker (1992–93)

They're like a bunch of cockroaches. It's not what they eat and tote off—it's what they fall into and mess up that hurts.

Darrell Royal

following the 14–9 upset loss to TCU in 1959
that ruined a perfect regular season for Texas.
Royal's often misunderstood comment was
said in frustration about the talented Horned
Frog team that played the role of spoiler

I heard [I'm] the answer to a question in Trivial Pursuit. I didn't believe it until somebody showed me the card from the game.

Chris Gilbert

the first running back in NCAA history
to rush for more than 1,000 yards three
straight seasons

I have often wondered what might have happened had I stayed at Texas. Maybe pro football never would have heard of Y. A. Tittle, or perhaps Bobby Layne's career would have been different. It's odd how fate steps in and changes the course of a man's life.

Y. A. Tittle

the Pro Football Hall of Fame quarterback who stayed at UT for several weeks in the summer of 1944, actually rooming with Bobby Layne and Rooster Andrews, before moving on to LSU, where his girlfriend was already enrolled

Today it's the most famous and hallowed uniform in Texas history, as much a part of Longhorn history as Bevo and Big Bertha. It has been worn by dozens, feared by thousands, coveted by countless, and even avoided by some. Winfred Tubbs, a promising linebacker on the 1992 team, was offered a chance to switch to No. 60 but declined because of the extra pressure that accompanied the jersey.

John Maher
Kirk Bohls

FAST FACT: Most prominently, Longhorns jersey No. 60 was worn successively by linebackers Johnny Treadwell (1960–62) and Tommy Nobis (1963–65). Later, All-Americans Britt Hager (1984–85, 1987–88) and Jeff Leiding (1980–83) were among those adorned by the jersey.

I see it on ESPN, and my memories start going. But if I'm an alumnus, I want to see No. 60 on the field tearing somebody's ass up rather than see it behind a pane of glass. That would give me more thrills. I just don't believe in that [jersey retirement] stuff.

Tommy Nobis
on the issue of whether or not to retire jersey
No. 60

G enerally we had a standing rule [about hair]. We wanted all of our guys to present themselves in a position where they could get a job out of college. So our hair rule had been they need to wear their hair like they are going to interview for a job. In Ricky Williams's situation, he interviews for a job every Saturday. So he was going to get work. So it wasn't as big an issue to me.

Mack Brown
on Williams's dreadlocks

Darrell said, "Well, what do you want me to do?" They said, "Say, yes." He said, "Well, of course I will! If that's what's holding us up, the meeting's over!"

"Mack" Rankin, Jr.
on Royal being asked to participate in a
meeting to consider the name change of
Texas Memorial Stadium to Darrell K. Royal
Texas Memorial Stadium

—◊◊◊—

When I'm old and looking back and gumming my food, it will be something that I will be really proud of.

Mack Brown
after winning the Big 12 title en route to the
national championship in 2005

TEXAS
NATIONAL CHAMPION ROSTERS

*L*onghorn followers no doubt experiencing the euphoria from the 2005 watershed season may feel no team in Texas history is its equal, but the Longhorns laid down some formidable teams under Darrell Royal in the 1960s that were dynastic in nature and powerhouse caliber in their dominance of opponents. These are the names from the glory years—Texas's three consensus national championship teams—and like all heroes who have fought the good fight, should never be forgotten: the champion Burnt Orange & White.

1963

11–0

(includes 28–6 Cotton Bowl victory over No. 2-ranked Navy)

Darrell Royal, *head coach*

	Pos	Wt	Ht	Yr	Hometown
Appleton, Scott	T	235	6–3	Sr	Brady
Bass, George	G	209	5–11	Sr	DeRidder, La.
Bedrick, Frank	C	201	5–10	So	Kaufman
Besselman, Jim	G	206	5–10	Sr	Corpus Christi
Boxwell, Mike	TB	185	6–1	So	Dumas
Bray, Clarence	C	191	5–11	Sr	Port Arthur
Brooks, James	T	235	6–3	So	Texas City
Brooks, Kenneth	E	201	6–2	So	Texas City
Brucks, George	G	201	6–0	Sr	Hondo
Buckalew, Charles	TB	175	5–8	Jr	Channelview
Carlisle, Duke	QB	176	6–1	Sr	Athens
Crosby, Tony	E/PK	190	6–1	Sr	Kountze
Currie, Tom	G	225	5–11	So	Houston
David, Jake	QB	174	6–1	So	Nederland
Derrick, Les	TB/QB	180	6–1	So	Houston
Dixon, Joe	WB	194	6–2	Jr	Dallas
Doerr, Timmy	FB	182	5–11	Jr	Cleburne
Echols, Charles	T	240	6–3	So	Rusk
Edwards, Fred	FB	185	5–10	So	Donna
Faulkner, Staley	T	225	6–3	Sr	Denton
Ferguson, Ken	T	217	6–0	Sr	Waco
Ford, Tommy	TB	183	5–9	Sr	San Angelo
Galiga, Joe	C	200	6–0	So	Hillsboro
Gaynor, Kim	WB	162	5–11	So	Fort Worth
Giles, Barney	G	185	5–11	So	Marshall
Goad, Howard	T	195	6–1	So	Cleburne
Green, Hix	TB	170	5–8	Jr	San Antonio
Halm, Kenneth	G	194	6–0	Sr	San Marcos
Harris, Phil	WB	195	6–0	So	San Antonio
Hensley, Lee	T	208	6–0	Jr	Henderson
House, Ben	E	180	5–10	Sr	Corpus Christi
Howe, Jack	C	217	6–2	So	Houston
Hudson, Jim	WB	205	6–2	Jr	LaFeria
James, Dwain	T	206	6–2	So	Lake Charles, La.
Kelley, Rodney	C	188	5–11	So	Weatherford
King, Anthony	WB	176	5–11	Jr	San Antonio
King, Mike	QB	160	6–0	So	Midland
Koy, Ernie	FB	206	6–2	Jr	Bellville
Kristynik, Marvin	QB	170	5–10	So	Bay City
Lacy, Clayton	T	196	5–11	Jr	Texas City
Lammons, Pete	E	195	6–1	So	Jacksonville
Landry, Ronny	E	195	5–11	So	Port Arthur
Mauldin, Dan	E	192	6–0	So	Azle
McWilliams, David	C	196	6–0	Sr	Cleburne
Nobis, Tommy	G	200	6–2	So	San Antonio
Nunnally, Knox	E	192	6–3	Jr	Midland
Philipp, Harold	FB	192	6–1	Jr	Olney
Price, Bo	G	200	6–2	Jr	Austin
Roberts, Gordon	T	220	6–1	Sr	West Lafayette, Ind.
Sands, Sandy	E	215	6–3	Sr	New London
Sauer, George	E	190	6–1	So	Waco

Unless otherwise noted, all hometowns are in Texas

Stockton, Tom	FB	186	6–0	So	Bryan
Talbert, Charles	E	201	6–5	Sr	Texas City
Talbert, Diron	T	205	6–5	So	Texas City
Underwood, Olen	G	208	6–3	Jr	Channelview
Wade, Tommy	QB	190	6–1	Sr	Henderson
Williamson, Pat	WB	185	6–3	So	Sour Lake

1969

11–0

(includes 21–17 Cotton Bowl victory over No. 9 Notre Dame)

Darrell Royal, *head coach*

	Pos	Wt	Ht	Yr	Hometown
Achilles, Jim	C	204	5–11	Jr	Spring Branch
Asaff, Tommy	HB	188	5–11	Sr	Marshall
Arledge, David	DE	177	5–11	So	Richardson
Atessis, Bill	DE	257	6–3	Jr	Houston
Ballew, David	HB	177	5–11	So	Clarksville
Banks, Andy	OT	228	6–0	So	Irving
Bertelsen, Jim	HB	197	5–11	So	Hudson, Wis.
Bolton, Jerrell	G	220	6–2	So	Granbury
Booher, Glen	DE	215	6–2	Sr	Oklahoma City, Okla.
Brooks, Leo	DT	244	6–6	Sr	Kermit
Callison, Bobby	FB	190	5–10	Jr	Abilene
Campbell, Mike	LB	186	5–11	Sr	Austin
Campbell, Tom	HB	183	5–11	Sr	Austin
Catlett, Bill	HB	186	6–0	So	Abilene
Cobb, George	DT	186	5–10	Sr	Amarillo
Collins, Terry	HB	181	5–6	Jr	San Angelo
Comer, Deryl	E	225	6–2	Sr	Dallas
Cormier, Jay	E	209	6–0	So	Freeport
Crawford, Charles	G	208	5–11	So	Spring Branch
Dale, Billy	HB	190	5–10	Jr	Odessa
Dean, Mike	G	195	6–0	Jr	Sherman
Ehrig, Ken	E	173	5–11	Sr	Gonzales
Feller, Happy	K	185	5–11	Jr	Fredericksburg
Frantzen, Glen	DT	225	6–1	Sr	Palestine
Fontenot, Raymond	LB	215	5–11	Jr	Port Arthur
Gunn, Jimmy	LB	180	6–0	So	Carrollton
Halsell, Glen	LB	202	5–11	Sr	Odessa
Henderson, Scott	LB	213	6–1	Jr	Dallas
Horn, Tim	FB	186	5–11	Sr	Lubbock
Hudgins, Buddy	LB	206	6–1	So	Ft. Worth
Huffman, Bob	DT	198	5–11	So	San Antonio
Hull, Jimmy	E	206	6–3	So	Pasadena
Hutchings, Mike	LB	191	6–0	Sr	Mt. Pleasant
Hutson, Kevin	HB	200	6–2	So	Littlefield
Johnston, Dickie	HB	190	6–0	Sr	Clovis, N.M.
Keasler, Syd	G	205	6–0	So	Hallsville
Keeton, David	HB	170	5–11	So	Houston
Kirk, Wayne	LB	200	6–1	So	Cameron
Koy, Ted	HB	212	6–2	Sr	Bellville
Kristynik, Paul	HB	174	5–9	Sr	Bay City
Lawless, Sam	HB	181	6–2	So	San Antonio
Layne, Rob	K	196	5–10	Sr	Lubbock
Lee, Tommy	HB	174	5–11	Jr	Amarillo
Lester, Danny	DB	215	6–2	So	Belton

Name	Pos	Wt	Ht	Yr	Hometown
Macha, Pat	DT	225	5–11	So	Orchard
Martin, Rick	LB	195	6–2	So	Odessa
Matula, Tommy	DT	223	6–4	So	Boling
Mauldin, Stan	DE	195	5–11	So	Azle
McBriety, Sam	OT	208	6–1	So	Ennis
McIngvale, George	C	229	6–3	So	Dallas
McKay, Bob	OT	245	6–6	Sr	Crane
McKinney, Mack	LB	195	6–3	Sr	Cameron
Mitchell, Bobby	G	206	5–11	Jr	Wheatridge, Colo.
Monzingo, Scooter	S	183	6–2	Sr	Del Rio
Nabors, Rick	HB	169	6–0	Jr	Austin
Otahal, Johnny	LB	194	6–0	So	Smithville
Paine, Robert	HB	182	5–11	So	Houston
Palmer, Scott	OT	224	6–2	Jr	Houston
Patman, Robbie	E	164	5–9	Sr	Texarkana
Phillips, Eddie	QB	188	6–0	So	Mesquite
Peschel, Randy	E	195	6–1	Sr	Austin
Ploetz, Greg	DT	205	5–10	Jr	Sherman
Richardson, David	LB	192	6–0	Jr	Abilene
Rike, Gary	HB	193	6–0	Sr	Dallas
Roach, Travis	DT	225	6–3	So	Marlin
Robichau, Paul	HB	189	5–10	So	Beaumont
Robinson, Johnny	HB	177	6–1	Jr	Plano
Rogers, Charles	G	206	6–2	So	San Antonio
Rushing, Jack	LB	198	6–0	So	Leaky
Schultz, Rob	DT	204	5–10	So	Cleveland, Tenn.
Speer, Mike	G	225	5–10	So	Rockdale
Speyrer, Cotton	E	169	5–11	Jr	Port Arthur
Squires, Rod	G	198	5–10	So	El Paso
Steinmark, Fred	S	166	5–10	Jr	Denver, Colo.
Stout, Randy	T	241	6–2	So	San Angelo
Street, James	QB	175	5–11	Sr	Longview
Terwelp, Dan	LB	192	6–3	So	San Antonio
Troberman, Rick	LB	175	5–9	So	San Antonio
Tyler, Ronnie	T	219	6–2	So	Jefferson
Webb, Larry	LB	198	6–1	So	Angleton
White, Carl	DT	216	6–4	So	McKinney
Wiegand, Forrest	C	200	6–1	Sr	Edna
Wiggenton, Donnie	QB	180	5–9	So	Spring Branch
Windham, Donny	HB	186	6–1	So	Post
Williamson, Jim	DE	198	6–0	Sr	Dallas
Woodward, Tommy	LB	201	6–1	So	Abilene
Worster, Steve	FB	208	6–0	Jr	Bridge City
Wuensch, Bobby	T	221	6–3	Jr	Houston
Young, Chris	DT	219	6–1	Sr	Houston
Zapalac, Bill	DE	206	6–4	Jr	Austin
Zapalac, Jeff	C	185	5–11	So	Austin

2005

13–0

(includes 41–38 Rose Bowl victory over No. 1 Southern Cal)

Mack Brown, *head coach*

Name	Pos	Wt	Ht	Yr	Hometown
Allen, Will	G	315	6–6	Sr	Houston
Andrade, Steven	DE	225	6–2	Sr	San Antonio
Areias, Sam	RB	201	5–7	Jr	Los Banos, Calif.
Aune, Coy	WR	195	6–2	So	Austin

Name	Pos	Wt	Ht	Yr	Hometown
Bailey, Ryan	K/P	180	6–2	Fr	Austin
Blalock, Justin	OT	329	6–4	Jr	Plano
Bobino, Rashad	LB	230	5–11	Fr	West Texas City
Bondy, Todd	LB	210	6–0	So	Southlake
Brown, Christopher	LB/DE	210	6–3	Fr	Texarkana
Brown, Tarell	CB	200	6–0	Jr	Mesquite
Buchanan, Will	QB	180	6–1	Fr	Austin
Campbell, Jeremy	LB	220	6–2	Fr	Richardson
Campos, Benjamin	PK	192	5–10	Jr	New Braunfels
Carter, Brian	WR	190	5–11	Sr	The Woodlands
Carvajal, Jaime	RB	147	5–4	So	Taft
Chareunsab, Xang	WR	155	5–8	Sr	Houston
Charles, Jamaal	RB	190	6–1	Fr	Port Arthur
Cosby, Quan	WR	200	5–11	Fr	Mart
Crowder, Tim	DE	270	6–4	Jr	Tyler
Derry, Scott	LB	230	6–3	So	Pearland
Dibbles, Larry	DT	285	6–2	Sr	Lancaster
Dockery, Cedric	G	315	6–4	Fr	Garland
Dolan, Greg	OT	290	6–7	Fr	Austin
Finley, Jermichael	WR/TE	220	6–5	Fr	Diboll
Flath, Michael	S	180	5–9	So	Arcadia, Calif.
Foreman, Eric	LB	230	6–4	So	Corrigan
Foster, Brandon	CB	180	5–9	So	Arlington
Fragoso, Adair	QB	215	5–11	Jr	El Paso
Garcia, Mike	G	315	6–3	Sr	Houston
Gatewood, Tyrell	TE/WR	210	6–2	So	Tyler
Gerland, Trevor	P	190	6–2	Fr	Katy
Griffin, Cedric	CB	205	6–2	Sr	San Antonio
Griffin, Dallas	C	275	6–4	So	Katy
Griffin, Marcus	S	195	6–0	So	Austin
Griffin, Michael	S	205	6–0	Jr	Austin
Hall, Ahmard	FB	235	5–11	Sr	Angleton
Hall, Chris	G	280	6–4	Fr	Irving
Hall, Eric	DE	245	6–2	Sr	Clarksville, Tenn.
Hardy, Myron	WR	210	6–2	So	Austin
Harvey, William	DS	212	5–11	Fr	Houston
Harris, Aaron	LB	230	6–0	Sr	Mesquite
Hills, Tony	OT	295	6–6	So	Houston
Hobbs, Antwaun	RB	180	5–7	Jr	Garland
Hofer, Mathew	RB	165	5–6	So	Austin
Hogan, Steven	TE	255	6–5	So	Sugar Land
Huff, Michael	S/CB	205	6–1	Sr	Irving
Jackson, Erick	CB	185	6–2	So	Cedar Hill
Jakes, Kaelen	DE	270	6–3	Sr	Valencia, Calif.
Janszen, Tully	DT	280	6–3	Jr	Keller
Johnson, Braden	LB	200	6–1	Sr	Euless
Johnson, Greg	P/PK	195	6–1	Jr	Lilburn, Ga.
Jones, Nate	WR	195	6–2	So	Texarkana
Kelson, Drew	LB	215	6–2	So	Houston
Kendall, Daniel	WR	185	6–2	Jr	Houston
Killebrew, Robert	LB	230	6–2	So	Spring
Kugler, Chad	LB	220	6–2	Fr	Richardson
Lane, Stephen	RB	185	6–0	Fr	Tyler
Lewis, Aaron	DE	275	6–4	Fr	Albuquerque, N.M.
Logan, Matt	WR	156	5–11	Sr	Houston
Lokey, Derek	DT	275	6–2	So	Denton
Marshall, Thomas	DT	293	6–6	So	Dallas
Martin, Marco	DT	355	6–3	Jr	Mesquite
McCoy, Colt	QB	195	6–3	Fr	Tuscola
McCoy, Mark	WR	188	6–2	Jr	Dallas
McCoy, Matthew	QB	195	6–3	Jr	Dallas
McGee, Richmond	P/PK	203	6–4	Sr	Garland
McWhorter, Mac	TE	226	6–4	Fr	Austin

Meijer, Karim	DB	200	5–10	Sr	Katy
Melton, Henry	RB	270	6–3	Fr	Grapevine
Melton, Matt	S	210	6–0	Jr	Flint
Michner, Cory	DE	210	6–0	Fr	St. Louis, Mo.
Miller, Roy	DL	300	6–2	Fr	Killeen
Moench, Ryan	DB	185	6–0	Fr	Austin
Moore, Justin	P	185	6–2	Fr	Houston
Muckelroy, Roddrick	LB	230	6–2	Fr	Hallsville
Myers, Marcus	RB	250	6–3	Jr	Austin
Nordgren, Matt	QB	235	6–5	Sr	Dallas
Oduegwu, Ishie	S	195	5–10	Fr	Denton
Ogbonnaya, Chris	RB	220	6–1	Fr	Missouri City
Okam, Frank	DT	315	6–5	So	Dallas
Orakpo, Brian	DE	238	6–4	Fr	Houston
Palmer, Ryan	DB	185	5–10	Fr	Arlington
Perez, Jason	LB	205	5–8	Sr	San Angelo
Peterman, Julian	LB	200	6–0	Fr	Schertz
Peters, Christoph	WR	220	6–3	Jr	Aachen, Germany
Phillips, Kyle	PK	192	5–11	Sr	Cypress
Pino, David	PK	180	5–8	Sr	Wichita Falls
Pittman, Billy	WR	198	6–0	So	Cameron
Poronsky, Brad	OT	290	6–7	Sr	Air Force Academy, Colo.
Portley, Kirby	TE	232	6–2	Sr	Kilgore
Ray, James	DB	190	5–9	Sr	Hewitt
Redwine, Nic	LB/DE	225	6–3	Fr	Tyler
Robison, Brian	DE	267	6–3	Jr	Splendora
Ross, Aaron	CB	192	6–1	Jr	Tyler
Schroeder, Nick	DS	240	6–2	Sr	The Woodlands
Schuldes, Roberto	LB	200	6–2	Fr	Modesto, Calif.
Scott, Jonathan	OT	315	6–7	Sr	Dallas
Sendlein, Lyle	C	305	6–5	Jr	Scottsdale, Ariz.
Shipley, Jordan	WR	184	6–0	Fr	Burnet
Solis, Jaicus	DT	250	6–4	Jr	San Angelo
Stavig, Cody	DB	195	5–10	Sr	Clackamas, Ore.
Studdard, Kasey	G	305	6–3	Jr	Lone Tree, Colo.
Sweed, Limas	WR	219	6–5	So	Brenham
Tanner, Charlie	C	280	6–4	Fr	Austin
Taylor, Michael	C	219	5–11	Fr	West Texas City
Taylor, Ramonce	RB/WR	195	5–11	So	Temple
Tefteller, Clayton	WR	175	6–0	Jr	Gilmer
Thomas, David	TE	245	6–3	Sr	Wolfforth
Tiemann, Luke	LB	219	6–2	So	Pflugerville
Torres, Freddy	QB	190	6–1	Fr	Pecos
Tweedie, Neale	TE	265	6–5	Jr	Lucas
Ulatoski, Adam	OT	290	6–8	Fr	Southlake
Ullman, Peter	TE	252	6–4	Fr	Austin
Valdez, Brett	C	305	6–4	Jr	Brownwood
Walker, George	WR	205	6–3	Fr	Houston
Winston, William	OT	345	6–7	Sr	Houston
Wright, Jerren	DB	164	5–10	Sr	Houston
Wright, Rodrique	DT	315	6–5	Sr	Houston
Young, Selvin	RB	215	6–0	Jr	Houston
Young, Vince	QB	233	6–5	Jr	Houston
Zepeda, Gilbert	QB	186	6–0	So	Pharr

BIBLIOGRAPHY

Bagnato, Andrew. "Longhorns, Trojans do Rose Bowl justice." *Arizona Republic,* 2006 Jan. 5: C1, C6.

Banks, Jimmy. *The Darrell Royal Story.* Austin, Texas: Shoal Creek Publishers, Inc., 1973.

Bianco, John, et al. *1998 Texas Football Media Guide.* Austin, Texas: University of Texas, 1998.

Bianco, John and Thomas Stepp. *2005 University of Texas Media Guide.* Austin, Texas: University of Texas, 2005.

Blanton, J. Neal. *Game of the Century: Texas vs. Arkansas, Dec. 6, 1969.* Austin, Texas: Jenkins Publishing Company, 1970.

Brown, Chip. "Texas' lone star wins it: Young rallies Longhorns to BCS title." *Arizona Republic,* 2006 Jan. 5: C6.

Clarkson, Rich, prod. *Texas Longhorn Football Today.* New York: Pindar Press, 1993.

Cromartie, Bill. *Annual Madness: Texas vs. Oklahoma.* West Point, N.Y.: Gridiron-Leisure Press, 1982.

Fleming, David. "Reggie Bush? Did You See Vince Young in the Rose Bowl?" *ESPN the Magazine,* 2006 Feb. 13: 63.

Frei, Terry. *Horns, Hogs, and Nixon Coming: Texas vs. Arkansas in Dixie's Last Stand.* New York: Simon & Schuster, 2002.

Hall of Legends Sports Series: *The Story of Darrell Royal.* Dir. Ryan Haidarian. Narr. Matthew McConaughey. Hall of Legends Sports Productions, 1998. 60 min.

Heard, Robert. *Oklahoma vs. Texas: When Football Becomes War, 1900–1980.* Austin, Texas: Honey Hill Publishing Co., 1980.

Layden, Tim. "Horns of Plenty." *Sports Illustrated,* 2005 Dec. 5: 50, 54.

Little, Bill. *Stadium Stories: Texas Longhorns.* Guilford, Conn.: Insider's Guide, 2005.

Maher, John and Kirk Bohls. *Bleeding Orange: Trouble and*

Triumph Deep in the Heart of Texas Football. New York: St. Martin's Press, 1991.

Maher, John and Kirk Bohls. *Long Live the Longhorns! 100 Years of Texas Football.* New York: St. Martin's Press, 1993.

Maysel, Lou. *Here Come the Texas Longhorns, 1893–1970.* Fort Worth, Texas: Stadium Publishing Company, 1970.

Neel, Eric. "Keeper: You Can't Stop Vince Young. The Longhorns Only Hope to Retain Him." *ESPN the Magazine,* 2005 Dec. 5: 52, 55, 56.

Richardson, Steve. *Tales from the Texas Longhorns: A Collection of the Greatest Stories Ever Told.* Sports Publishing L.L.C., 2003.

Royal, Darrell with John Wheat. *Coach Royal: Conversations with a Texas Football Legend.* Austin, Texas: University of Texas Press, 2005.

Schoor, Gene. *100 Years of Texas Longhorn Football.* Dallas, Texas: Taylor Publishing Company, 1993.

Shaw, Gary. *Meat on the Hoof: The Hidden World of Texas Football.* New York: St. Martin's Press, 1972.

Stratton, W. K. *Backyard Brawl: Inside the Blood Feud Between Texas and Texas A&M.* New York: Crown Publishers, 2002.

WEB SITES

Associated Press. "Late score lifts Texas to second straight Big Ten win." http://sports.espn.go.com/ncf/recap?confId=&gameId=252530194, Sept. 10, 2005.

Associated Press. "Young leads Texas to first OU win in five years." http://sports.espn.go.com/ncf/recap?gameId=252810251&confId=null, Oct. 9, 2005.

Associated Press. "Tech suffers first loss this season with 52–17 pounding." http://sports.espn.go.com/ncf/recap?gameId=252950251, Oct. 23, 2005.

Associated Press. "QB Young excited about contest with Ohio State." http://sports.espn.go.com/ncf/preview?gameId=252530194&confId=null&date=20050910, Sept. 10, 2005.

Associated Press. "Longhorns survive scare at Oklahoma State." http://sports.espn.go.com/ncf/recap?gameId=253020197, Oct. 29, 2005.

Associated Press. "Longhorns blank Baylor to remain undefeated." http://sports.espn.go.com/ncf/recap?gameId=253090239, Nov. 5, 2005.

Associated Press. "Young gets Texas offense record in rout of Kansas."

http://sports.espn.go.com /ncf/recap?gameId=253160 251, Nov. 12, 2005.

Associated Press. "Young, Longhorns struggle, but pull away to top Aggies." http://sports.espn.go.com /ncf/recap?gameId=253290 245, Nov. 25, 2005.

Associated Press. "Young, Bush top NCAA award winners." http://www.thestar.com /NASApp/cs/Content Server?pagename=thestar/ Render&c=Article&cid=1134 082212088&call_pageid=968 867503640, Dec. 8, 2005.

mackbrown-texasfootball.com. "Derrick Johnson." http://www.mackbrown-tex-asfootball.com/pages/bios04 /johnson_derrick.html.

Davis, Brian and Chip Brown. *Dallas Morning News.* "All-Time Red River Shootout Team." http://www.dallas-news.com/sharedcontent/ dws/spt/colleges/redriver-shootout/stories/100704dns porralltime.21c2dc7a.html, Oct. 6, 2004.

Forde, Pat. ESPN.com. "Mack won't admit it, but OU win one to enjoy." http://sports.espn.go.com /espn/columns/story?colum nist=forde_pat&id=2185121, Oct. 9, 2005.

Forde, Pat. ESPN.com. "Texas playing like No. 2 team . . . for now." http://sports.espn.go.com /espn/columns/story?colum

nist=forde_pat&id=2201018, Oct. 24, 2005.

Forde, Pat. "USC, Texas should dominate postseason awards." ESPN.com. http://sports.espn.go.com /espn/columns/story?colum nist=forde_pat&id=2252258, Dec. 8, 2005.

Forde, Pat. "Goal down, dream to go for Longhorns." ESPN.com. http://sports.espn.go.com /espn/columns/story?colum nist=forde_pat&id=2246572, Dec. 3, 2005.

Forde, Pat. "Six unsung talents key Texas offensive attack." ESPN.com. http://sports.espn.go.com /espn/columns/story?colum nist=forde_pat&id=2273788, Dec. 30, 2005.

Forde, Pat. "Longhorns, Brown finally knock down title door." ESPN.com. http://sports.espn.go.com /espn/columns/story?colum nist=forde_pat&id=2281000, Jan. 4, 2006.

Griffin, Tim. ESPN.com. "Longhorns' 2005 rise mir-rors 1969 title run." http://sports.espn.go.com /ncf/news/story?id=2234723, Nov. 23, 2005.

Griffin, Tim. "Mack Brown looking for first conference title." ESPN.com. http://sports.espn.go.com /ncf/news/story?id=2241989, Dec. 2, 2005.

Hanley, Reid. "Vince-stant classic; Young drives Texas to 5 TDs, winning field goal in thriller; TEXAS 38 MICHIGAN 37." *Chicago Tribune.* http://proquest.umi.com. dewey.phoenixpubliclibrary.o rg:2048/pqdweb?did=772956 421&sid=4&Fmt=3&clientId=1082&RQT=309&VName=PQD, Jan. 2, 2005.

Little, Bill. "Bill Little commentary: Honoring a champion." mackbrown-texasfootball.com. http://www.mackbrown-texasfootball.com/index.php?s= &url_channel_id=41&url_su bchannel_id=&url_article_id =1255&change_well_id=2, May 7, 2002.

Little, Bill. "Bill Little commentary: A stable of horses." mackbrown-texasfootball.com. http://www.mackbrown-texasfootball.com/index.php?s= &url_channel_id=41&url_su bchannel_id=&url_article_id =1415&change_well_id=2, Aug. 17, 2005.

Maisel, Ivan. "Special teams lift unbeaten Horns past Aggies." ESPN.com. http://sports.espn.go.com /ncf/columns/story?columnist=maisel_ivan&id=223674 6, Nov. 25, 2005.

Maisel, Ivan. "Brown delivers after change of attitude." ESPN.com. http://sports.espn.go.com /ncf/bowls05/columns/story

?columnist=maisel_ivan&id= 2272247, Dec. 28, 2005.

Rasizer, Lee. "Nalen can see finish line with Broncos." *Rocky Mountain News,* http://www.rockymountainnews.com/drmn/broncos/ article/0,1299,DRMN_17_39 77044,00.html, Aug. 4, 2005.

Sherrington, Kevin. "UT raising receiving standards." *Dallas Morning News,* http://dodgeglobe.big12.net /stories/102200/tex_102200 8136.shtml,Oct. 22, 2000.

Simmons, Bill. "Welcome back, Coach Fredo." Page 2, ESPN.com. http://sports.espn.go.com /espn/page2/story?page= simmons/060105, Jan. 5, 2005.

Vertuno, Jim. "Young, No. 2 Texas beat No. 24 Colorado." Associated Press. http://www.usatoday.com/sp orts/college/football/games /2005–10–15-colorado-texas_x.htm, Oct. 15, 2005.

Vertuno, Jim. "Young shows flashes of old self, then returns to stellar form." Associated Press. http://sports.yahoo.com /ncaaf/news;_ylt=AoWM-CoK9YvQLdi5rVBlUErccvr YF?slug=ap-t25-texas-young &prov=ap&type=lgns, Oct. 24, 2005.

INDEX